Contents

Introduction 4

Natural History of the Phylum *Mollusca* 5

Collecting Shells 7

Cleaning Shells 8-9

Anatomical Drawings 10-11

Location Map 12

Glossary 13-15

The Gastropods 16-75

Chitons, Tusk Shell, Nautiluses, Spirula 76-77

The Bivalves 78-105

Index 106

Introduction

The descriptive text and the color photographs are intended to give prominent and easily identifiable characteristics to aid in the identification of each mollusk. However, in attempting to identify specimens, the shell collector must learn to expect some amount of variation in color, size, patterns, and shape from the statistics given in this book. Size measurements are of average, mature shells that are most likely to be found. Shape is often quite variable between adult and juvenile snails, and environmental surroundings can affect the size and shape of the shells. Water temperature, diet, water currents and turbidity, foreign growths, can all affect development. Those shells that live and mature in quiet waters are more likely to be larger and more fragile than those in exposed wave-washed areas. Abnormalities in development are not uncommon, and in many cases contribute to the value of the specimen. For example, a right-handed specimen of the normally left-handed lightning whelk is rare; or an albino individual of a normally colorful species may be more highly prized.

More than 6000 species of mollusks are found in American waters. Those included in these accounts are the ones most likely to be found in the littoral zone or in shallow waters, or those that are particularly favored as collector's specimens because of size, color, or beauty. The gastropods and bivalves are arranged in order of evolutionary development within their class, starting with the most primitive or earliest species. Re-evaluation of scientific names of species occurs constantly; those used are the most recent and generally accepted classifications, but references to former or other classifications are included.

Along with the description of each mollusk, the value of the shell is included. Obviously, even the first shell collectors, thousands of years ago, wondered what the shells they found were worth—either in terms of barter, food value, practical use, or adornment. American Indians of the northeast coast made wampum from hard shell clams, whelks, and periwinkles; Indians living on the Pacific coast of the United States used tusk shells as currency. The values listed are intended to be a guide to the price you can expect to pay or get when buying or selling shells. Obviously, prices on individual shells of the same species will vary depending on size, condition, scarcity and demand. However, some uncommon shells may not be worth much if they are not particularly attractive or interesting; and some usually common shells may demand a surprising price because of their size or because they are heavily collected and in demand. Therefore, consider the listed prices a guideline, knowing full well that you may be asked to pay more, and may pay it, for that shell you simply *must* have in your collection.

The Complete Collector's Guide to

Shells & Shelling

Sandra Romashko

*Sea Shells from the Waters of the
North American Atlantic and Pacific Oceans,
Gulf of Mexico, Gulf of California,
The Caribbean, The Bahamas, and Hawaii*

𝒲𝒾𝓃𝒹𝓌𝒶𝓇𝒹 Publishing, Inc.

105 NE 25th St. P.O. Box 371005 Miami, Fl. 33137

2nd Edition

3 5 7 9 10 8 6 4
Printed in the United States of America.
Library of Congress Catalog Card No. 81-51067
ISBN 0-89317-032-1

Natural History of Phylum *Mollusca*

Members of this group are casually classified as "shelled animals". The shell is the product of the mantle, a thin sheet of muscular flesh which envelopes the vital organs of the animal and in some species can cover the back and sides of the shell like a skirt. The mantle has many pores through which the animal secretes a thin limy substance which solidifies quickly into a thin layer. Layers are built up one upon the other, often crosswise, until the mass is built up into the shell. Often, the surface is "final coated" by the animal with a thin porcelain-like finish. The outer edges of the mantle continue to secrete, allowing the shell to grow in width and length, while pores in the mantle within the shell add to the thickness of the shell and also perform any necessary repairs.

In some species the interior walls are made of alternating layers of lime and horny tissue—shingle-like lime crystals. When light is reflected from the edges of these microscopic shingles, the luster produced is known as mother-of-pearl.

In addition to the mantle, the body of the mollusk also consists of the head, the foot, and visceral mass. The head is well developed and distinct in the snails and squids, but is not defined in the bivalves. Also, the gastropods have a ribbon-like set of teeth known as the radula in the mouth cavity, which is absent in the bivalves. Within the visceral mass are contained the circulatory, respiratory, reproductive, digestive, and excretive organs. Waste ducts from the paired kidneys and intestine open into the mantle cavity. Mollusks have a two-chambered heart that circulates colorless or blue blood. Most have separate sexes, but there are many hermaphroditic species. Most mollusks reach their mature size in one to six years.

Six Classes of the Phylum *Mollusca*

1. The class *Monoplacophora* contains primarily extinct fossil species—there are only five living deep-sea species. They are limpet-like in shape, have paired internal organs and gills, lack eyes and tentacles, and have a single row of radular teeth.

2. The chitons, class *Amphineura*, have a shell made up of eight plates enclosed by a leathery border, the girdle, which holds the plates in place. They have a large broad foot, a head that lacks eyes and tentacles but has a well-developed radula. They are sluggish, preferring shallow water where they adhere to rocks by means of the flat foot. Sexes are separate; most are herbivorous, but some species are carnivores.

3. Univalves or snails belong to the class *Gastropoda,* which has the greatest number of members of the entire phylum. These animals have a single shell, which is usually coiled or cap-like; some are shell-less. They have a distinct head, most with a radula, two eyes and well-developed tentacles, and many have an

operculum. Representatives of this class can be found in salt or fresh water, or on land as air-breathing animals. The aquatic species have gills and the land snails have a modified "lung". Univalves can be either herbivorous or carnivorous; many are hermaphroditic, and some have sex reversal.

4.   The class *Pelecypoda* includes the bivalves, which have a pair of shells joined by a hinge and held together by strong internal muscles. A head is lacking, but the animal feeds upon minute plant and animal matter which is drawn into the shell through one siphon and expelled through another siphon. There is a muscular foot which is used for burrowing, or for attachment to rocks or coral by the immobile species. All of the members of this second-largest class of mollusks are aquatic, and most are marine species. In most species the sexes are separate, but some like the scallops are hermaphroditic, and still others have sex reversal.

5.   Tusk shells are in the class *Scaphopoda*. These elongated mollusks have long tapered conical shells which are slightly curved and open at both ends. They live buried in mud with the small end of the shell sticking up into the water. The larger, posterior end contains a foot; there is no true head, but eyes, gills and radula exist. The sexes are separate in this exclusively marine group.

6.   Another entirely marine class, *Cephalopoda*, includes the squids, octopuses, nautiluses, and spirulas. These are highly specialized invertebrates which are extremely fast, have good vision, and all have a head with a parrot-like beak which is surrounded by long prehensile tentacles covered by suckers. The majority of the species are predators; the sexes are separate.

Collecting Shells

While occasionally a beautiful shell specimen will be washed up onto a beach by a gentle wave, coastal areas will more likely be strewn with broken and bleached shells. Most prized specimens are obtained by collecting live mollusks. Since they are primarily nocturnal, with the aid of a bright light mollusks can be effectively sought at night on beaches during low tide. Beachcombing during daylight can produce results, but rocks will have to be overturned, crevices and protected areas inspected, and natural covers of seaweeds and grasses scrutinized. Divers with the aid of a snorkel will find that exploring shallow waters will be productive. In any case, an experienced eye will contribute to success, since live specimens are likely to be camouflaged by algae and marine growths and hidden by other invertebrates and their surroundings.

Caution—some areas and waters are protected by federal or state laws. It is imperative that the shell collector find out about any regulations protecting mollusks and reefs. And even if the area is not protected, the shell collector has an obligation to protect and restore the habitat—do not disturb the environment any more than absolutely necessary, replace any rocks or cover that was moved, and *don't over collect!*

Dredging is a productive way to collect specimens from sandy bottoms. A small, hand-made dredge can be dragged from the stern of a rowboat or small motor boat. The dredge should be fairly small so that it can still be hauled when it is weighted to dig into the muddy bottom. And while they may not be obvious during dredging, small specimens may be included in the mud that collects in the dredge. Some of the matter should be saved, dried and inspected for tiny prizes.

Cleaning Shells

LIVE SPECIMENS

If the specimen was collected alive, the flesh must be cleaned out before it deteriorates and produces offensive odors. There are several ways to clean out live shells.

1. Put the shell in cool salt or fresh water and gradually bring to a boil. Boil gently for about five minutes, so as not to damage the shell. Most of the snails can then be hooked and removed by unwinding them; the shells of the bivalves will gape, allowing easy removal of the fleshy matter.

2. Some can be cleaned alive. If the animal is slightly extended, pierce the muscle with the tines of a fork and pull the animal out with a sharp twist and jerk.

3. Larger snails can be frozen for a few days and then defrosted. The soft parts should then be removed and the cavity flushed thoroughly with water.

4. Heavy specimens can be hung by the foot, until the weight of the shell pulls the animal out.

5. In warmer areas, the shell can be burried in dirt for a few days so that ants and other insects can clean out the flesh. Or bury the shell in soft, dry sand, where it will rot out after several days. If allowing the snail to rot, be sure the aperture is down so that the shell will not be stained by the decaying matter.

6. Preserve live specimens in a 50% solution of methyl or isopropyl alcohol. After about a week, the animal can be easily removed. Or, small shells preserved in alcohol need only be dried.

7. Small, fragile shells can be soaked in water for 2-3 days unitl the flesh has rotted out. Water should be changed frequently during this period.

8. The specimen can also be preserved in formalin. The use of formalin makes it unnecessary to remove the body since the procedure dries and hardens the flesh. You may however choose to remove the matter anyway. Soak the shell in a 5% solution of formalin. The formaldehyde solution which is available from drug stores is a 40% solution; mix 1 part with 8 parts water for the proper solution. The dilute formaldehyde solution must be buffered with 1 teaspoon sodium bicarbonate (baking soda) per quart of solution. Soak for several days, after which the animal should be easy to remove.

EMPTY SHELLS

After the shell is rid of all the animal matter, it may still require cleaning to remove growths or deposits.

1. In many cases scrubbing the shell in warm, soapy water will clean it sufficiently. If you choose to keep the periostracum on your specimen, this is the only additional cleaning method you should use since bleach or other stronger solutions will dissolve the periostracum. Also, do not subject the operculum to any other cleaning solutions.

8

2.   Soaking the shell in commercial laundry bleach will remove algae and other stains. The soaking time and concentration of bleach can be increased for heavily stained shells.

3.   Shells can also be soaked in a strong lye solution. This will also remove stains and growths, but in addition it will loosen calcareous deposits which can then be carefully chipped away.

4.   A muriatic acid solution can be used to clean heavily encrusted shells, but this is not recommended unless absolutely necessary. The acid reacts with the encrustations on the shell, but it also will react with the shell itself, leaving a hole in the shell or even dissolving the specimen. The shells should be immersed in the muriatic acid for only short periods of time, and thoroughly rinsed after each soaking.

After any cleaning method, be sure that the shell is rinsed thoroughly or soaked in fresh water. Any residual chemical can still react with the shell and possibly mar or even destroy it. And, of course, protect your hands and arms from any caustic or acid solution—use forceps or tongs to immerse and remove shells from the cleaning baths.

In all circumstances, be sure to save the operculum so that it can be replaced inside the aperture after the shell has been cleaned and dried. This can be done by gluing the operculum to a wad of cotton and placing it in the opening of the shell.

Bivalves must be cleaned carefully so as not to break the hinge. Clear glue or shellac lightly applied to the hinge will strengthen it. After cleaning, a bivalve can be soaked in a solution of equal parts of glycerine and water and tied shut until dry, which will allow the shell to stay shut; dead bivalves will normally be in the open position.

Once the shells have been cleaned they can be beautifully displayed almost anywhere—but they should be kept from sunlight since their color will soon be bleached out. If you choose, apply a light coating of neatsfoot oil to enhance the finish and color.

CHITONS

Preparing chitons as specimens requires special treatment, otherwise they roll up into tight balls. The animals should be kept alive in sea water. Put the chiton on a piece of wood or glass in a dish of sea water. When it is in a flattened position, hold the chiton down with your thumb on its back and at the same time pour out the water and replace with a 70% solution of alcohol. After a couple of minutes, the chiton will remain flat; let it soak for a few days.

Once the chiton is preserved and dried, the fleshy parts can be removed. Do not damage or remove the girdle, which holds the plates in place.

If you prefer to remove the eight plates, clean and reassemble them, simply boil the chiton in water for about five minutes and follow by soaking in household bleach for another 30 minutes. Any tissue can now be removed from the plates with a stiff brush. After drying, the plates can be glued together again. The cleaned plates will have a range of colors from white to blue-green with markings of yellow, orange or pink.

GASTROPOD SHELL

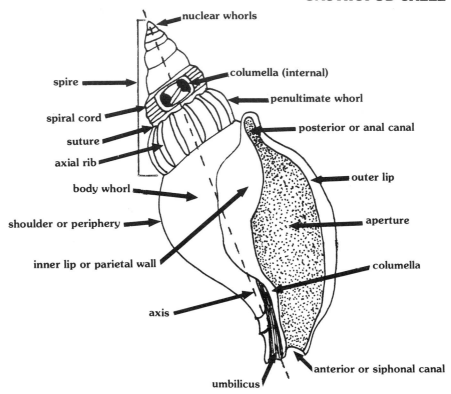

nuclear whorls

columella (internal)

spire

penultimate whorl

spiral cord

posterior or anal canal

suture

axial rib

outer lip

body whorl

shoulder or periphery

aperture

inner lip or parietal wall

columella

axis

anterior or siphonal canal

umbilicus

BIVALVE SHELL

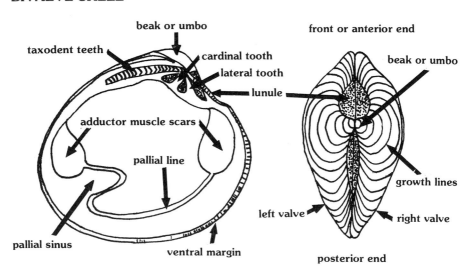

beak or umbo

front or anterior end

taxodent teeth

cardinal tooth

beak or umbo

lateral tooth

lunule

adductor muscle scars

pallial line

growth lines

pallial sinus

left valve

right valve

ventral margin

posterior end

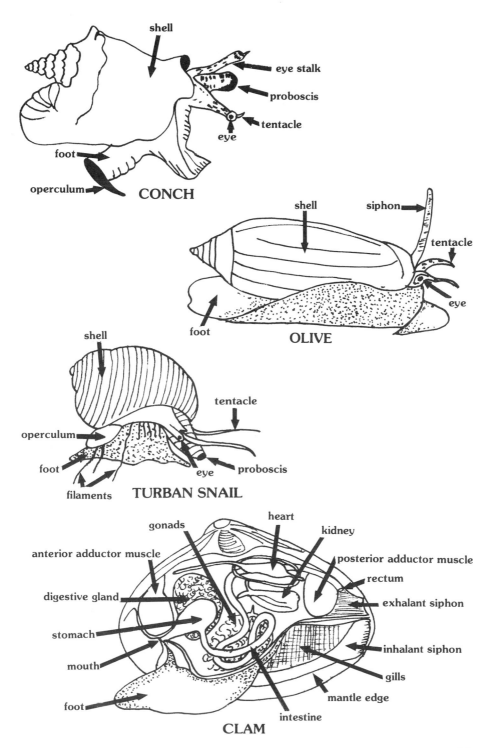

CONCH
- shell
- eye stalk
- proboscis
- tentacle
- eye
- foot
- operculum

OLIVE
- shell
- siphon
- tentacle
- eye
- foot

TURBAN SNAIL
- shell
- tentacle
- operculum
- foot
- eye
- proboscis
- filaments

CLAM
- gonads
- heart
- kidney
- anterior adductor muscle
- posterior adductor muscle
- rectum
- digestive gland
- exhalant siphon
- stomach
- mouth
- inhalant siphon
- gills
- foot
- mantle edge
- intestine

11

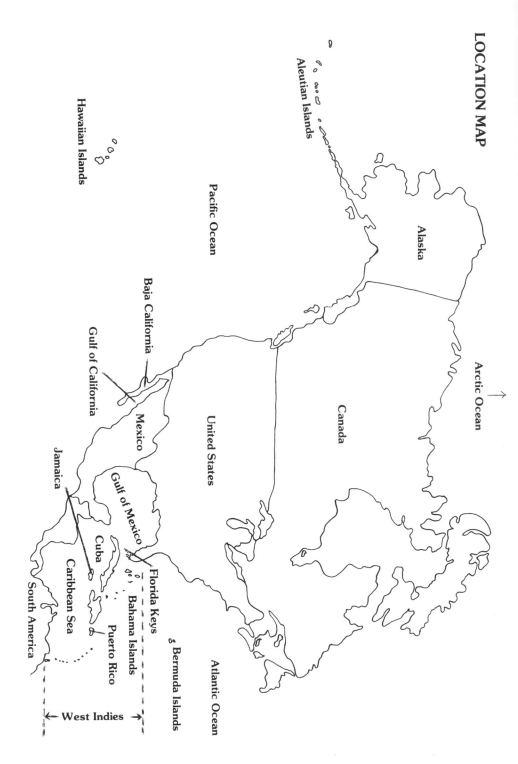

LOCATION MAP

Aleutian Islands

Hawaiian Islands

Pacific Ocean

Alaska

Arctic Ocean

Baja California

Gulf of California

Mexico

United States

Canada

Jamaica

Gulf of Mexico

Cuba

Caribbean Sea

Puerto Rico

Florida Keys

Bahama Islands

Bermuda Islands

Atlantic Ocean

South America

← West Indies →

12

Glossary

adductor muscle   in bivalves, the one or two large muscles within the shell that open and close the two valves

anterior end   in bivalves, the front end where the foot protrudes from the shell

aperture   in gastropods, the opening in the last whorl which permits the foot and head of the animal to extend from the shell

apex   in gastropods, the tip of the spire; in tusk shells, the small, open hind end

beak   in bivavles, the umbo, the earliest formed part of a valve, usually above the hinge

body whorl   in gastropods, the last and largest whorl of the shell

byssus   in bivalves, a bundle of hair-like strands which is used for attaching the shell to rocks, ledges, coral, etc.

calcareous   made of calcium carbonate; shelly, limy

callus   in gastropods, a calcareous deposit, such as enamel covering a portion of the shell

canal   in gastropods, the open channel on the outer lip or at the base of the shell through which the siphon protrudes

cardinal teeth   in bivalves, the largest two or three shell ridges in the hinged portion of the valve, just under the beak

carnivorous   feeding on animal flesh

chink   lengthened groove along the columella

chondrophore   in bivalves, the spoon-shaped shelf in the hinge which contains the cartilaginous resilium

columella   in coiled gastropods, the solid or hollow axis or pillar around which the whorls are formed

cord   a coarse spiral line on the surface of the shell

dextral   turning from left to right; right handed; aperture on right side of axis

foot   in gastropods, a muscular organ used for locomotion, adhering to a surface, or digging

gape   the space between the valves of a bivalve when they are only partially closed

girdle   in chitons, a band of leather-like muscular tissue that surrounds the valves and holds them together

herbivorous   feeding on plant matter, algae

hermaphrodite   mollusk which functions as and has the organs of both sexes

inequivalve   in bivalves, the sizes of the two shells are not the same

intertidal zone   the area between the high- and low-tide lines; littoral zone

involute   in gastropods, rolled inward from each side

lateral teeth   in bivalves, long, narrow shelly ridges located in the hinge, below the cardinal teeth

left valve   in bivalves, the shell that is on the left when the whole mollusk is viewed on end with the beak facing you and the anterior end up

ligament   in bivavles, an external or internal band of cartilage, usually behind the beaks, that holds the shells together

littoral zone   the area between the high- and low-tide lines; intertidal zone

lower valve   in bivalves, the more deeply cupped of the two shells

lunule   in bivalves, a depressed heart-shaped area located in front of the beaks

mantle   a fleshy organ that encases the vital organs of the mollusk; it usually contains the glands that secrete the shell

margin   the edges of the shell

nacre   the layer of shell which is pearly or iridescent; mother-of-pearl

nuclear whorl   in gastropods, the earliest or first whorl of the shell

operculum   in gastropods, a shelly or horny plate which completely or partially covers the aperture

outer lip   in coiled gastropods, the outer margin of the aperture farthest from the columella

pallial line   in bivalves, scar on interior of shell where mantle was attached

parietal sheild   in gastropods, a shelly thickening or deposit on the parietal wall; parietal callus

parietal wall   in gastropods, the part of the body whorl opposite the outer lip and bordering the upper part of the aperture; the inner lip

penultimate whorl   in gastropods, the next to the last whorl of the shell; the whorl just above the body whorl

periostracum   smooth or fibrous layer which covers all or part of the hard calcareous shell

periphery   in gastropods, the part of the whorl bulging out from the axis

plates   in chitons, the eight hard valves which make up the shell; dorsal shield

posterior end   in bivalves, the hind end where the siphons protrude from the shell

proboscis   a tubular extension of the head having a mouth at the end

radula   an organ located in the mouth cavity composed of minute teeth which may or may not be attached by a flexible ribbon-like muscle, which is used for feeding

resilium   in bivalves, a horny, pad-like cushion located internally in the hinge which causes the shell to spring open when the muscles are relaxed

ribs   lines in the surface of mollusk shells—axial in gastropods and radial in bivalves

right valve   in bivalves, the shell that is on the right when the whole mollusk is viewed on end with the beak facing you and the anterior end up

sculpture   indented or raised markings on the surface of the shell

sessile   permanently attached, unable to move about

shoulder   in gastropods, a flattened part of the whorl below the suture

sinistrial   turning from right to left; left-handed; aperture on left side of axis

siphon   tube-like extension of the mantle which carries water and waste in and out of the mantle cavity

spire   in gastropods, collectively all the whorls above the body whorl

suture   in spiral gastropods, the line or space where one whorl touches another

thread   a fine line in the surface of the shell

umbilicus   in gastropods, a small hollow at the base of the columella which is visible from below

umbo (pl. **umbones**)   in bivalves, the beak or prominent part of the shell above the hinge

upper valve   in bivalves, the flatter of the two shells

valve   in bivalves, one of the two parts of the shell; in chitons, one of the eight plates that make up the dorsal shield

varix (pl. **varices**)   in gastropods, an axial line or ridge that marks the former location of the outer lip, caused by a thickening of the lip during a major growth stoppage

veliger   the most developed larval stage of mollusks which can be egg encased or free swimming

visceral mass   the fleshy body matter of the mollusk which includes the abdominal organs

whorl   in gastropods, a turn or coil in the shell

wing   in bivalves, a flattened projection from one or both sides of the hinge line

Class: *Gastropoda*

Abalones (family: *Haliotidae*)
Abalones have very small spires, the majority of the shell being the body whorl. There are four to six natural holes along the left margin which are used by the animal to expel water and waste. The inside of the shell has an iridescent or pearl-like appearance, often multicolored. The abalones are commonly found in shallow water, but can be found in depths to 1200 ft. (366 m), clinging to rocks and other underwater growth with such surprising tenacity that they must be removed with the aid of a pry bar. All are edible; in fact, they are so heavily fished that state laws control harvesting and restrict legal size of possession. The size of the abalones ranges up to 12 in. (305 mm) and they can live 15-20 years.

corrugated or **pink abalone,** *Haliotis corrugata* Wood The color of this shell varies from dark green to reddish brown and is characterized by strong ribbing, 2-4 high-rimmed holes, and the scalloped edge; inside is mother-of-pearl. It is found among seaweeds in moderately shallow water from southern California to Baja California. It is a fairly common species and is 6-10 in. (152-254 mm) in length. $10

green abalone, *Haliotis fulgens* Philippi The thick, greenish-brown to brown shell has 5-7 open perforations and prominent, closely-spaced spiral ribs. Interior is blue-green to pink mother-of-pearl. Uncommon due to over-harvesting, it is found in southern California to Baja California in moderately shallow water and is 6-8 in. (152-203 mm) long. $9-$18

red abalone, *Haliotis rufescens* Swainson This reddish-brown species is one of the largest of our abalones, reaching 10 in. (254 mm) or more. The heavy shell is sometimes encrusted and has 3-4 open holes along the margin and a red edge along the outer rim; interior is pale. It is found on rocks in moderately shallow water along the U.S. Pacific coast from Washington to Baja California. The red abalone is fairly common, and is the most commercially important of the abalones. $3-$10; over 9 in. (229 mm) $100-$125

Keyhole Limpets (family: *Fissurellidae*)
Keyhole limpets are conical-shaped shells with an oval-shaped base, and a hole at the apex in the adult. Young specimens have a slit in the anterior edge of the shell, but the slit fills as growth proceeds until the slit is a hole in the top of the adult shell. The keyhole or slit is used to expel water and waste, corresponding to the holes in the shell of the abalone. Keyhole limpets feed at night on algae-covered rocks in the intertidal zone. Most species are vegetarians, but some are carnivores.

rough keyhole limpet, *Diodora aspera* Eschscholtz The gray to yellowish shell often has dark radial rays; interior is plain white with a callus around the hole. A common species, found on rocks from the low-tide line to moderately shallow water along the west coast of the U.S. from southern Alaska to Baja California. It is 1-2 in. (25-50 mm) long. $1-$2

Lister's keyhole limpet, *Diodora listeri* d'Orbigny Found on rocks at the low-tide line, Lister's limpet is dirty white to gray with prominent radial ribs forming a rough exterior. Common throughout Florida to the West Indies, the shell may reach 2 in. (50 mm) in length. under $1-$2

corrugated abalone

green abalone

red abalone

Lister's keyhole limpet

rough keyhole limpet

Keyhole Limpets (continued)

Barbados keyhole limpet, *Fissurella barbadensis* Gmelin Distinguished from other limpets by the green interior, the shell has many prominent irregular ribs, varying in color from gray to purplish. A very common species from south Florida to the West Indies and to Brazil, the ¾-1½ in. (20-40 mm) long shell is found in the intertidal zone, but is often covered with algae and may go unnoticed. under $1

white keyhole limpet, *Fissurella gemmata* Menke Previously classified as *F. alba*, Carp. A narrow black rim encircles the thick callus around the hole, while the external color is white or light gray. It is a common shell, little more than 1 in. (30 mm) long, and is found in shallow water in the southern Gulf of California. $2-$3

knobby keyhole limpet, *Fissurella nodosa* Born The exterior of the shell is grayish to brownish with strong radial ribs and a prominently notched margin. A common species, ¾-1½ in. (20-40 mm) long, it is found throughout Florida to the West Indies on rocks just below the low-tide line. under $1-$2

great keyhole limpet, *Megathura crenulata* Sowerby This largest known keyhole limpet reaches a length of 4 in. (102 mm) and has a keyhole approximately one-sixth of its length. The animal has a dark gray to black mantle which is large enough to cover the entire shell. The shell is brownish and the keyhole is encircled in white. A common edible species, it is becoming more scarce due to over harvesting. Found in shallow water on rocks from the low-tide line out, and on breakwaters from central California to Baja California. $2-$4

True Limpets (family: *Acmaediae*)

True limpets have a conical shell without any hole or slit. The height and shape of the shell is influenced by the environment: those in exposed areas and subject to heavy wave action have low shells; those that adhere to seaweeds have more elongated shells. Most species inhabit the intertidal area where they feed, at night among rocks, on microscopic plant life. They may reach 4 in. (102 mm) across and they move by means of a single broad muscular foot. Limpets are eaten in some places.

file limpet, *Acmaea limatula* Carpenter Also listed as *Collisella limatula*. The mid-height oval shell is dark, greenish black and about 1 in. (25 mm) across. It is commonly found on rocks in the intertidal zone on the Pacific coast from Puget Sound to Mexico. under $1-$2

black limpet, *Cellana exarata* Nuttall The oval, moderately arched shell is marked with distinct black radiating ribs with lighter color between the ribs. It reaches a length of 1½ in. (38 mm) and is found among rocks near

shore in Hawaii—where it is also sold in fish markets as *opihi*. Common. under $1

giant owl limpet, *Lottia gigantea* Sowerby This largest North American true limpet, reaching 3-4 in. (76-102 mm) in length, is named for the bluish "owl-shaped" markings on the interior of the shell. The slightly arched oval shell is mottled brown or gray-black with a rough surface. It is common on rocks between tide lines on coasts from California to Mexico. The foot is edible $1-$2

Barbados keyhole limpet

white keyhole limpet

knobby keyhole limpet

great keyhole limpet

file limpet

giant owl limpet

black limpet

Top Shells (family: *Trochidae*)

These shells are largely composed of iridescent mother-of-pearl which may be concealed on the outer shell by various pigmentations, but the insides retain the pearly luster. They have a thin horny operculum which is made up of many whorls. Top shells are vegetarians, feeding by means of many radulae. They range in size from ⅛-6 in. (3-150 mm) across and are found among rocks and seaweed in shallow water or, some species, in great depths.

top shell, *Calliostoma bonita* Strong, Hanna & Hertlein A small, tan shell found on the Pacific coast, primarily in Baja California, it reaches less than 1 in. (24 mm) across. This species lives on kelp beds, offshore; fairly common. $1-$2

channeled top shell, *Calliostoma canaliculatum* Lightfoot The thin strong shell ranges in color from a yellowish tan to a rich brown. This fairly common shell is found in seaweeds offshore on the Pacific coast from Alaska to southern California. It attains 1½ in. (38 mm) in length. $2-$9

sculptured top shell, *Calliostoma euglyptum* A. Adams Dingey white, mottled with red and brown, this shell is found along the Atlantic coast from North Carolina to Florida and around to Texas. Found in sand in shallow to moderately deep water, this common species has a strong shell about 1 in. (25 mm) high. $4-$18

Calliostoma iris Pilsbry This small cream-colored shell is found off Florida's east coast. Fairly common, it reaches ½ in. (13 mm) across. $3

chocolate-lined top shell, *Calliostoma javanicum* Lamarck Previously classified as *C. zonamestum,* A. Adams. A tan colored shell with 5-7 fine, chocolate-brown lines, it is about 1 in. (25 mm) across. This rather rare species is found from southern Florida to the West Indies in coral sand in shallow water. $6-$18

jujube top shell, *Calliostoma jujubinum* Gmelin Shell color varies from brown to red, with white specks above the suture; it reaches 1 in. (25 mm) in height. Fairly common in its range along the Atlantic coast from North Carolina to Florida and to the West Indies. It inhabits seaweeds and sand in shallow water and is commonly washed up on sandy shores. $1-$4

western ribbed top shell, *Calliostoma ligatum* Gould This solid, brown shell has rounded whorls and 6-8 large tan threads. Its range extends from Alaska to California, and it is found in shallow water among stones and algae. A common shell, it is usually under 1 in. (25 mm) high. $1-$5

granulose top shell, *Calliostoma supragranosum* Carpenter A glossy, pale brown shell, some specimens are beaded near the sutures, others have white spots. Usually less than ½ in. (13 mm) high, they are found among rocks in the intertidal zone from Monterey, California to Baja California. Fairly common. $2

West Indian top shell, *Cittarium pica* Linné Previously classified as *Livona pica.* A heavy, rough shell, it is marked with purplish-black and white zigzag markings. The horny operculum is round and greenish blue in live animals. A large shell, it can attain 4 in. (102 mm) in height. It is found in shallow water among rocks in the intertidal zone in the West Indies. Specimens may be found in southern Florida, but it is extinct there; it is also found in old Indian shell mounds. Common in West Indies. under $1-$4; over 3 in. (76 mm) $15

superb gaza, *Gaza superba* Dall This is a shiny, yellowish-gray shell, with the last whorls a lighter straw color with a pinkish sheen. The light, but strong shell has rounded whorls and reaches 1-1½ in. (25-38 mm) across. Found in deep water from the Gulf of Mexico to the West Indies, it is not easy to obtain but is found by dredging. $40-$50

top shell

sculptured top shell

channeled top shell

Calliostoma iris

jujube top shell

chocolate-lined top shell

western ribbed top shell

granulose top shell

West Indian top shell

superb gaza

Top Shells (continued)

vortex margarite, *Margarites vorticiferus* Dall   This is a low shell with rapidly expanding whorls and many circular threads. It is pinkish to brown, ⅜-⅞ in. (10-22 mm) across. Common, found offshore in deep water from Alaska to southern California. $1-$2

channeled solarielle, *Solariella lacunella* Dall   A very small shell, ⅛-⅜ in. (3-10 mm), it is thick, white to pearl gray and the whorls have six spiral cords, and the top three are beaded. Common, found in sand or rubble in shallow to moderately deep water from Virginia to Key West, Florida. $4-$5

smooth Atlantic tegula, *Tegula fasciata* Born   Color is extremely variable, from yellowish to grayish pink and mottled with red, brown, black. About ½ in. (13 mm) high, the shell is smooth and sometimes shiny, and there may be two teeth at the base of the columella. Common, found in shallow water under rocks in its range from south Florida to the West Indies.   under $1-$2

rough top shell, *Tegula rugosa* A. Adams About ¾ in. (19 mm) across, this solid shell is mottled gray, sometimes with pink markings and occasionally dark bars on a pinkish background. It is a common shell, found in the Gulf of California in moderately shallow water. $1-$2

Star Shells and Turbans (family: *Turbinidae*)

Members of this family are solid, heavy shells and have a strong calcareous operculum. The shells are top shaped, the surface is generally brightly colored but the texture varies and can be smooth or spiny. They feed in shallow water on marine algae and are primarily a tropical family.

star arene, *Arene cruentata*   Mühlfeld A small shell, easily identified by the 4-5 sharply angled whorls with prominent triangular spines, it is about ½ in. (13 mm) across and ¼ in (6 mm) high. The outside is white, flecked with red or brown and the operculum is covered with tiny beads. This uncommon shell is found under rocks in shallow water from southeast Florida to the West Indies. $1-$10

American star shell, *Astraea americana* Gmelin   Also listed as *A. tecta americana.* About 1 in. (25 mm) high, the shell has a pointy apex. It is whitish, heavy, and the 7-8 whorls have axial riblets. The white operculum usually has an indentation. Common, found in grass and under rocks in shallow water at low tide in southeast Florida. $1-$2

vortex margarite

channeled solarielle

smooth Atlantic tegula

rough top shell

star arene

American star shell

carved star shell, *Astraea caelata* Gmelin
Conical in shape and a strong shell, the carved
star shell reaches 3 in. (76 mm) in height. The
rough outer surface is greenish white, mottled
with red, and has both prominent oblique ribs
and revolving ribs. The heavy operculum is
whitish and calcareous. It is a common shell,
found in shallow water among coral rubble and
reefs in southeast Florida and the West Indies.
$2-$5

long-spined star shell, *Astraea phoebia*
Röding Previously classified as *A. longispina,* Lamarck. Yellowish to pale tan in color,
this shell is 1-2½ in. (25-64 mm) across, and low,
only about half as high. It is characterized by
the triangular spines that project from the shell.
A common species, found in grassy shallows in
southeast Florida to the West Indies. under
$1-$8

star shell, *Astraea phoebia spinulosa* Röding
Previously classified as *A. longispina spinulosa,* Lamarck. This shell is a sub-species of the
long-spined star shell, the primary variation
being the length of the spines, which are
shorter on *A. p. spinulosa.* Common, found
in grassy shallow water from southeastern
Florida to the West Indies. under $1-$2

green star shell, *Astraea tuber* Linné
The solid, rough shell is about 1½ in. (38 mm)
high, greenish brown with irregular white
blotches and has wide, obliquely vertical ribs.
It is common in shallow water on coral reefs in
southeast Florida to the West Indies. There is a
limy operculum. $1-$3

channeled turban, *Turbo canaliculatus*
Hermann This shell is composed of about 5
well-rounded whorls sculptured with spiral
cords. It is named for the strong channeled
suture. The smooth finish is checked with
green and brown over a lighter greenish-yel-
low-tan background. It has a heavy operculum
and reaches 2-3 in. (50-76 mm) in height. It is not
common, found in moderately shallow water in
the Florida Keys and West Indies. $5-$15

chestnut turban, *Turbo castaneus* Gmelin
The tan beaded surface of this shell is marked
with darker brown blotches; occasionally, specimens may have spines and/or be dull green.
The shell is solid, has 5 or 6 whorls and is about
1½ in. (38 mm) high. It is common, found in shallow waters from North Carolina to Florida and
Texas, and to the West Indies. $2-$4

Turbinidae

carved star shell (juvenile)

carved star shell

star shell

long-spined star shell

channeled turban

green star shell

chestnut turban

Nerites (family: Neritidae)

Nerites are common tropical shells which are usually found in shallow water among rocks; but they can also be found in brackish water, fresh water, or even on dry land. The shells are small, usually colorful, and generally round in shape.

bleeding tooth, *Nerita peloronta* Linné The common name is well suited, based on the appearance of the aperture which has white teeth surrounded by an orange stain. It can be found among rocks where the animal feeds at night on algae. The 1-1½ in. (25-38 mm) high shell is common from southern Florida to the West Indies. under $1-$6

tessellate nerite, *Nerita tessellata* Gmelin Another easy to identify nerite, the color is checked dirty white and black; in rare cases it may be all black. The small shell, ½-¾ in. (12-19 mm), has a dark operculum. Common, in intertidal zone from Florida to Texas and to the West Indies. under $1

four-toothed nerite, *Nerita versicolor* Gmelin The whitish shell is marked with black and red splotches and the inner lip usually has four white teeth. About 1 in. (25 mm) high, the thick porcelain-like shell has a grayish, pimply operculum. Common on rocks in intertidal waters from Florida to the West Indies. under $1

netted nerite, *Neritina piratica,* Russell A small shell, less than ¾ in. (20 mm) high, it has a smooth yellowish or olive-green surface covered with a network of closely placed black lines resulting in a dotted design. Common, found in brackish water in the West Indies. under $1

virgin nerite, *Neritina virginea* Linné Usually less than ½ in. (13 mm) high, this shiny, tiny shell occurs in a variety of colors and markings. The inner lip has small irregular teeth; the operculum is smooth. It is very common in brackish water from Florida to Texas and to the West Indies. under $1-$2

zebra nerite, *Puperita pupa* Linné This white shell has many black stripes across its surface. It is small, ½ in. (13 mm) high, has a pale yellow operculum and the aperture is yellow to orange. It is commonly found in rock pools just above the high-tide line throughout southern Florida and the West Indies. under $1

Periwinkles (family: Littorinidae)

This large family has worldwide distribution and is littoral, occupying varied habitats including rocks, grasses, pilings, roots. Different species can tolerate long periods without water and a wide range of water salinity. The sexes are separate; the penis of the male is prominent and the shape is distinctive enough to aid in identification of the various species. Periwinkles have a chitinous, large operculum which completely covers the aperture when the snail is withdrawn. They feed on microscopic plant life which they scrape up by means of hundreds of rasp-like teeth arranged in rows on the long ribbon-like radula. Periwinkles excrete a trail of mucus along their paths, and the head bears a well-developed pair of tentacles, each with an eye at the base.

false prickly-winkle, *Echininus nodulosus* Pfeiffer The heavy shell has its whorls marked with revolving rows of pointed knobs and is mottled gray in color. The 1 in. (25 mm) shell is common and found above the high-tide line from Florida to the West Indies. $1

southern periwinkle, *Littorina angulifera* Lamarck Color of this thin but strong shell is variable. It may be gray, reddish, purplish, or rarely, yellow or orange. The shell has a horny operculum and is about 1¼ in. (31 mm) high. This is a common species and can be found on mangrove roots, leaves, and pilings in shallow water from southern Florida to the West Indies. under $1

bleeding tooth

netted nerite

false prickly-winkle

tessellate nerite

four-toothed nerite

zebra nerite

virgin nerite

southern periwinkle

Periwinkles (continued)

common European periwinkle, *Littorina littorea* Linné This smooth thick shell is usually brownish to nearly black, spirally banded with numerous dark bands. The shell is ½-1½ in. (13-38 mm) high with 6 or 7 whorls. It is extremely common from Labrador to Maryland and in Europe, where it is a favorite food, often sold roasted in the shell by street vendors. It is believed to be a recently introduced species to the eastern Atlantic Ocean, but specimens more than 1000 years old have been found in Indian mounds in Nova Scotia. It is found on rocks and in seaweed in the intertidal zone. The female lays eggs in a horny egg capsule which disintegrates and the young hatch in about a week. under $1

cloudy periwinkle, *Littorina nebulosa* Lamarck The grayish to yellow shell is occasionally marked with brown spots, and smaller shells often have cloud-like brown and white splotches—the basis for the common name. The ⅝-1⅛ in. (16-28 mm) high shell is found on rocks at the low-tide line in its range, Florida to Texas and the West Indies. under $1

northern yellow periwinkle, *Littorina obtusata* Linné This small, smooth shell has virtually no spire. It has 4 whorls, the last is so large that the other whorls scarcely rise above. About ½ in. (13 mm) high, the color is variable, primarily yellow, but it can be orange or brownish yellow, and sometimes banded. It is a common shell, found on seaweed in the intertidal zone from Labrador to New Jersey. under $1

northern rough periwinkle, *Littorina saxatilis* Olivi Color is variable, the shell can be yellowish, gray to dark brown, and some young specimens can be spotted with yellow or black. About ½ in. (13 mm) high, it has numerous spiral ridges. Common, found on rocks in the intertidal zone, and often above the water line. It is found on both U.S. coasts from Alaska to Puget Sound, and the Arctic Sea to New Jersey. under $1-$2

zigzag periwinkle, *Littorina ziczac* Gmelin Whitish with many dark brown or black wavy fine lines; a rare specimen can be blue-gray. It is common, found among rocks in intertidal zone from southeast Florida to the West Indies. under $1

common prickly periwinkle or **prickly winkle,** *Nodilittorina tuberculata* Menke This shell is brown and has 5 whorls with several rows of small pointed knobs. It is a common shell, about ¾ in. (19 mm) high, and is found on rocks in the intertidal zone from southern Florida to the West Indies. under $1

beaded periwinkle, *Tectarius muricatus* Linné Grayish, with many spiral rows of small regular white beads, this top-shaped shell is about ¾ in. (19 mm) high. It lives on rocks from the high tide mark to well out of water. The species can live for long times without water. It is common from the Florida Keys to the West Indies. under $1

common European periwinkle

cloudy periwinkle

northern rough periwinkle

northern yellow periwinkle

zigzag periwinkle

common prickly periwinkle

beaded periwinkle

Turrets (family: *Turritellidae*)

A large family with many prized and colorful members, turrets are primarily Pacific shells, but a few species are found in Atlantic waters. The shells are long and slender, and may be tightly or loosely coiled.

boring turret shell, *Turritella acropora* Dall Also listed as *Torcula acropora*. The shell can be whitish, pale yellow, or pinky brown, with brown mottlings, and is 1-1½ in. (25-38 mm) long. It is a fairly common species, usually found by dredging moderately shallow water. Its range is from North Carolina to Florida and to the West Indies. $1-$2

Cooper's turret shell, *Turritella cooperi* Carpenter Also listed as *Haustator cooperi*. This slender shell is about 1½ in. (38 mm) long, and is yellowish or light orange, usually with brown streaks. The aperture is normally round. It is fairly common, found in sand in moderately shallow water below the tide line from Monterey to San Diego, Cal. $1-$15

eastern turret shell, *Turritella exoleta* Linné A long slender shell, the eastern turret is creamy white splashed with brown splotches and can attain a length of 3 in. (76 mm). It is a common species, found in moderately shallow to deep water, from southern Florida to the West Indies. $1-$9

turret shell, *Turritella gonostoma* Valenciennes The largest western American species, this turret has a strong heavy shell and reaches a length of 6 in. (152 mm). It is bluish gray and heavily marked with brown splotches; there are about 20 flat whorls with fine spiral cords. The shell is fairly common, found in moderately shallow water from the Gulf of California to Peru. $1-$6

Knorr's worm shell, *Vermicularia knorri* Deshayes The tight, early whorls—the "turritella stage"—of this species are white, while the rest of the loose whorls are yellow-brown. It reaches a length of 3 in. (76 mm), and is common, found primarily among sponges in shallow water. The range of this shell is from North Carolina to the West Indies. $2-$4

common worm shell, *Vermicularia spirata* Philippi The turritella portion is white or brown, with the rest of the irregular shell being yellow to reddish brown. It reaches a length of 6 in. (152 mm) and is often found growing with sponges or in colonies intertwined with other individuals. In spite of its appearance, it is a true gastropod, having tentacles, eyes and radula on the head at the end of the elongated body. The common worm shell is found in shallow waters from Massachusetts to Florida and to the West Indies. under $1

Sundials (family: *Architectonicidae*)

This family is characterized by the broad umbilicus about which coiled whorls give the circular but not elevated shape. Sundials start life as sinistral, left-handed, larvae, but the nuclear whorls end up hidden at the bottom of the umbilicus as the shell grows and the new whorls coil in the same direction and grow over the apex resulting in a right-handed shell.

common sundial, *Architectonica nobilis* Röding The circular shell is somewhat flattened and 1-2 in. (25-51 mm) in diameter and about ¾ in. (19 mm) high. It is white or gray with brown and purple spots. The whorls have several strong spiral cords, and are beaded in the early whorls. It is fairly common and found in shallow water in sand on both coasts: from North Carolina to Florida and Texas and to the West Indies and Brazil, and also Baja California to Peru. It is often found washed ashore. $1-$4

keeled sundial, *Architectonica peracuta* Dall A rather small sundial, ¾ in. (19 mm), it is whitish or light gray. Uncommon, found from southern Florida to the Gulf of Mexico and to the West Indies. $10-over $50

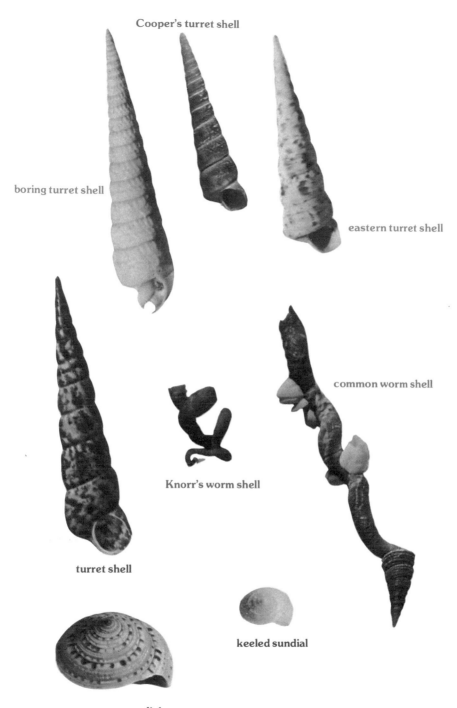

Cooper's turret shell

boring turret shell

eastern turret shell

common worm shell

Knorr's worm shell

turret shell

keeled sundial

common sundial

turrets / sundials

Slit Worm Shells (family: *Siliquariidae*)

These shells have an open slit along the length of irregular loose coils that allows water to enter the mantle cavity.

slit worm shell, *Siliquaria squamata* Blainville Previously classified as *Tenagodus squamatus,* Blainville. This 5-6 in. (127-152 mm) species is grayish to light yellow with the early whorls being smooth and having spines on the later whorls. They are found in sponges in moderately shallow water from North Carolina to Florida and the West Indies. $10

Modulus (family: *Modulidae*)

The porcelain-like shells resemble miniature top shells. The base of the columella ends in a sharp tooth-like spine.

Atlantic modulus, *Modulus modulus* Linné The yellow-white shell is marked with brown and has low revolving ridges with deep grooves separating the vertical ribs. It is ½-¾ in. (12-17 mm) in diameter, very common in shallow water on eelgrass from North Carolina to Florida and Texas and to the West Indies. It is quite variable in appearance. under $1-$2

Horn Shells (family: *Potamididae*)

These are mud dwellers and have elongated, many whorled shells and a horny round operculum.

California horn shell, *Cerithidea californica* Haldeman A heavy shell about 1½ in. (38 mm) long, it is dark brown, usually with thin white or yellowish bands and strong axial ribs on the whorls. Common, on mud flats from Bolinas Bay, Cal. to Baja California. $1-$2

horn shell, *Cerithidea montagnei* d'Orbigny A shiny, chocolate-brown shell, usually with paler bands on the whorls, it is about 1½ in. (38 mm) long. Large aperture has a flaring outer lip, and the whorls have sharp ribs. Found in mud in shallow water, it is common from the Gulf of California to Ecuador. $1-$2

Wentletraps (family: *Epitoniidae*)

The family has over 200 species, yet almost all are whitish and extremely similar in appearance. They are carnivores, feeding on anemones, corals, coelenterates.

lamellose wentletrap, *Epitonium lamellosum* Lamarck A long slender shell ⅝-1¼ in. (16-32 mm) long, it is whitish with some irregular brownish markings. The 7-8 whorls have numerous blade-like ribs. Common from southern Florida, West Indies; Hawaii. $1-$5

brown-banded wentletrap, *Epitonium rupicola* Kurtz Small, usually less than 1 in. (25 mm) high, the shell is white or yellowish, usually with 2 brown bands. Common, in sand from low-tide line to moderately deep water from Cape Cod, Mass. to Florida and Texas. $1-$6

Janthina Snails (family: *Janthinidae*)

The members of this family are usually violet, pelagic, and float on the surface buoyed by a mass of bubbles.

common purple sea snail, *Janthina janthina* Linné A fragile shell, 1-1½ in. (25-38 mm), it is light purple above the periphery, darker below. Fairly common, worldwide; in U.S., south from Nantucket and San Diego; Hawaii. under $1-$2

Slipper Shells and Cup-and-saucer Limpets (family: *Calyptraeidae*)

These shells are cap shaped with a shelly shelf or cup on the underside which supports some of the fleshy parts of the animal. They lack an operculum.

common Atlantic slipper shell, *Crepidula fornicata* Linné The convex shell can be strongly arched or limpet-like, is light colored, flecked with light brown spots and is about 1½ in. (38 mm) across. On the underside, the shelf covers almost one-half of the shell. Common, found among rocks and on other shells in moderately shallow water from Nova Scotia to Florida and Texas, and introduced off the state of Washington. $1

West Indian cup-and-saucer, *Crucibulum auricula* Gmelin A whitish or grayish cap-shaped shell, 1 in. (25 mm) in diameter, and the cup is virtually free standing. Uncommon, usually found attached to other shells from North Carolina to Florida, West Indies. under $1-$2

Carrier Shells (family: *Xenophoridae*)

These flattened top-shaped shells cement piece of shells, coral and stones to their own shells, so that they look like small piles of debris.

Atlantic carrier shell, *Xenophora conchyliophora* Born The unencumbered shell is 1-3 in. (25-76 mm) across, yellowish, but generally covered by attached objects projecting from the lower edge of the whorls. Uncommon, found on sand near rubble and coral reefs in moderately shallow water from southern Florida to the West Indies and Brazil. $3-$24

Caribbean carrier shell, *Xenophora caribaeum* Petit This thin-shelled large species reaches 3½ in. (89 mm), is whitish, and it only attaches a few small bits to its shell at the suture line. Uncommon, in deep water from the Florida Keys to the West Indies. $15-$25

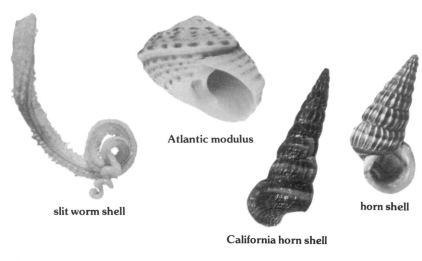

Atlantic modulus

slit worm shell

horn shell

California horn shell

lamellose wentletrap

brown-banded wentletrap

common purple sea snail

West Indian cup-and-saucer

common Atlantic slipper shell

Atlantic carrier shell

Caribbean carrier shell

slit worm shell / modulus / horn shells / wentletraps / janthina snail
slipper shell / cup-and-saucer limpet / carrier shells

Conchs (family: *Strombidae*)

True conchs are active snails which have a heavy, solid shell with a greatly enlarged body whorl and claw-like operculum which does not close up the aperture. The expanded outer lip is characteristically notched at the lower end—the "stromboid notch". The last two whorls of the pointed spire have rows of spines. The conchs feed on algae and are found among sea grasses in sand or rocks.

Florida fighting conch, *Strombus alatus* Gmelin   The solid shell has about 7 whorls, has a pointy spire and is 3-4 in. (76-102 mm) long. It is yellow-brown, marked with orange and purple mottlings or bands, and the interior is dark brown. Juveniles and immature specimens lack the flaring lip and strongly resemble cone shells. The spire has short spines and the outer lip slopes downward, differentiating it from the West Indian fighting conch. This is a common species, found in shallow water in grassy, sandy areas from North Carolina to Florida, Gulf of Mexico and Texas, and to the Yucatan. $1-$3

milk conch, *Strombus costatus*   Gmelin The thick, heavy, white or yellowish shell is covered by a thin periostracum which is easily removed when the shell is dried. The milk conch is 4-6 in. (101-152 mm) long, has heavy knobs on the body whorl; inside of the shell and lip are whitish. This fairly common shell is found in shallow water in grassy, sandy bays and lagoons. Its range is from southeastern Florida to the West Indies and to Mexico. $5-$10; pink $12-$25; lavender $30; albino $50

rooster-tail conch, *Strombus gallus*   Linné The heavy shell is mottled brown, white and orange, has a sharp spire and has blunt nodes at the shoulders on the body whorl. This uncommon shell reaches a height of 4-7 in. (102-178 mm) and is found in moderately shallow water from southern Florida to the West Indies. $7-$35

queen conch or **pink conch,** *Strombus gigas* Linné   This large, heavy shell is yellowish white, irregularly marked with brown and is 7-12 in. (178-305 mm) high. Fresh specimens have a thin periostracum which is easily removed when the shell is dried. Most of the shell is the body whorl, and in adults the outer lip is thick and greatly flaring. The spire is short and conical, and there are blunt nodes on the shoulders; interior of shell is bright pink. Juveniles lack the flaring lip and are marked with zigzag brown stripes. The pink conch is one of our largest gastropods and is heavily fished commercially. Found on sandy, grassy bottoms in shallow water, it is normally a common shell, but it is becoming scarcer due to overfishing for food and souveniers. Its range is from southern Florida to the West Indies. $4-$45; albino $85

West Indian fighting conch, *Strombus pugilis* Linné   The deep yellow-brown shell reaches a height of 3-5 inches (76-126 mm) and has an orange aperture. The later whorls have prominent spines and the outer lip slopes upward which differentiates it from the Florida fighting conch. Its range is from southeastern Florida to the West Indies where it is common in shallow water. $3-$12

hawk-wing conch, *Strombus raninus* Gmelin The yellow-white shell is marked with brown streaks and blotches, has a well developed spire, thick and greatly flaring lip with a deep notch near the bottom. It is 4-5 in. (102-127 mm) high and the shoulders of the body whorl have nodes. It is a common species, found in shallow water from southern Florida to the West Indies. $2-$8

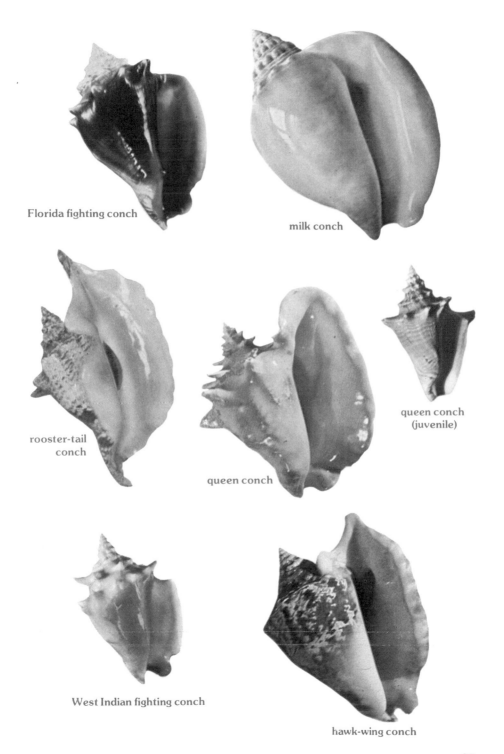

Florida fighting conch

milk conch

rooster-tail
conch

queen conch

queen conch
(juvenile)

West Indian fighting conch

hawk-wing conch

Cowries (family: *Cypraeidae*)

These highly polished, colorful shells are oval-shaped and have a thick-lipped aperture marked with teeth on both sides; no operculum. Immature specimens are fragile and lack the curled lip and are usually banded, whereas the adult is spotted.

Atlantic deer cowry, *Cypraea cervus* Linné
Our largest cowry, it can reach 7 in. (178 mm) in length. Similar in appearance to the measled cowry, except the deer cowry is more inflated, has a thinner shell, and the small whitish spots lack brown centers. The heavily spotted brown shell has brown apertural teeth. Fairly common in shallow water, Florida to West Indies. $3-$25; over 5 in. (127 mm) $6-$145

Atlantic gray cowry, *Cypraea cinerea* Gmelin   A round, plump cowry, the top is grayish brown diffusing to lilac, sides are spotted with blackish-brown dots or streaks. The bottom is white, apertural teeth are small; shell is 1½ in. (38 mm) long. Fairly common, in shallow water, Florida to West Indies. $1-$5

mouse cowry, *Cypraea mus* Linné   This rather uncommon species is 2 in. (51 mm), tan overall with darker wavy lines and is speckled; outer lip has brown teeth. Found in southern Caribbean. $6-$25; over 1¾ in. (44 mm) $30-$50

chestnut cowry, *Cypraea spadicea* Swainson   The back of the whitish shell has a large, light chestnut brown spot outlined by an irregular dark brown margin; it is 1-2½ in. (25-64 mm). The narrow aperture is white and both lips have teeth. Fairly common, from below the low-tide line to moderately deep water from Monterey, Cal. to Baja California. $2-$25

Atlantic yellow cowry, *Cypraea spurca acicularis* Gmelin   This cowry has strong white teeth on both sides of the aperture, the base is white and the back is yellowish orange with many white and brown spots; ¾-1¼ in. (20-32 mm) long. Uncommon, found on shallow-water reefs from South Carolina to Florida, West Indies. $3-$6

measled cowry, *Cypraea zebra* Linné   The highly polished dark brown cowry has white spots with those on the sides having brown centers. It is 2-4½ in. (51-114 mm) long and has brown apertural teeth on both lips. Young specimens have broad bands which occasionally remain in the adult. Fairly common, found in shallow water from southeast Florida to the West Indies. $6-$30

Trivias (family: *Eratoidae*)

Similar in appearance to true cowries, trivias are smaller and characterized by the small ribs which run around the shell from the narrow aperture to the center of the back.

apple seed erato, *Erato vitellina* Hinds   Small, about ½ in. (13 mm) long, it is wider at one end, giving it a pear-like appearance. The shell is brown, blotched with purple. The thickened outer lip bears small teeth. Common, in shallow water from California to Mexico. $2-$4

coffee bean trivia, *Trivia pediculus* Linné   The ⅜-¾ in. (10-19 mm) long trivia is tan to violet-brown, with three pairs of irregular brown blotches on the back. Common, found on coral reefs in shallow water from Florida to the West Indies.   under $1-$2

four-spotted trivia, *Trivia quadripunctata* Gray   Pink with 1-4 brownish dots on both sides of the median furrow, this shell is about ¼ in. (6 mm) long. Common in shallow water from Florida to the West Indies. $1-$5

suffuse trivia, *Trivia suffusa* Gray   The pink shell usually has faint blotches and the riblets are beaded at the median furrow. Less than ¼ in. (6 mm) long, it is common in shallow water from south Florida to the West Indies. $1-$2

Simnia and Cyphoma Snails (family: *Ovulidae*)

Glossy, slender shells, the members of this family live on sea whips and sea fans (*Gorgonia sp.*). Each species of *Cyphoma* has a characteristically colored and patterned mantle. It is believed that the colored simnias take on the color of the sea fans they inhabit.

single-toothed simnia, *Neosimnia uniplicata* Sowerby   Commonly pink or purple, it can be white or yellow. The thin shell is ¾ in. (19 mm) long and the long narrow aperture ends in a blunt point. Common, from North Carolina to the West Indies. $2-$7

flamingo tongue, *Cyphoma gibbosum* Linné   The solid shell has a dorsal hump across the center of the shell, is about 1 in. (25 mm) long, white or yellowish with orange edges and is highly polished. Common, from North Carolina to the West Indies.   under $1-$2

McGinty's cyphoma, *Cyphoma mcgintyi* Pilsbry   About 1 in. (25 mm) long, whitish with lavender tints, the shell is very similar to the flamingo tongue, but McGinty's cyphoma is more elongated and the hump is somewhat narrower. Somewhat uncommon, found in shallow water from the Florida Keys to the Bahamas. $4-$5

Atlantic deer cowry

Atlantic gray cowry

mouse cowry

Atlantic yellow cowry

chestnut cowry

measled cowry

apple seed erato

coffee bean trivia

four-spotted trivia

suffuse trivia

single-toothed simnia

flamingo tongue

McGinty's cyphoma

Moon Shells (family: *Naticidae*)

Extremely active carnivores, the moon snails feed on bivalves, eating as many as three or four clams a day. The snail digs out its prey from under the sand and pierces the shell with the radula and glandular acid, forming a hole through which the flesh is sucked up. The foot of the animal is so large that when extended it often conceals the entire shell. The operculum can be either horny or calcareous.

colorful Atlantic natica, *Natica canrena* Linné The almost-round smooth shell is 1-2½ in. (25-64 mm) high, is yellowish white with spiral rows of brown spots, stripes, and zigzag markings. The limy operculum has numerous spiral grooves on the exterior side. Moderately common, found in sand in shallow water from North Carolina to Florida and to the West Indies. $1-$6

livid natica, *Natica livida* Pfeiffer Small, glossy gray shell, it has a white band below the suture and darker spiral bands on the body whorl; aperture is brown. The shell is ¼-¾ in. (6-19 mm) high, and has a white calcareous operculum. Fairly common, found on sand flats in shallow water from southern Florida to the West Indies. under $1-$4

Morocco natica, *Natica marochiensis* Gmelin About ½-1 in. (13-25 mm) high, the shell is grayish brown with a narrow white band below the suture and spiral bands of lightly defined reddish-brown spots on the body whorl. The operculum is calcareous. Common, in sandy shallow water from southeastern Florida to the West Indies. $3-$5

shark's eye, *Polinices duplicatus* Say The large shell, 2-3 in. (50-76 mm) high, is smooth, solid, gray to tan in color and usually wider than it is high; operculum is horny. A common shell, it is found on sand and mud flats in shallow water from Cape Cod, Mass. to Florida, Gulf of Mexico, Texas. $1-$8

brown moon shell, *Polinices hepaticus* Röding Previously classified as *P. brunneus*, Link. The thick shiny shell can be tan or orange-brown, and attains 1½ in. (38 mm) in height. Operculum is horny; aperture is white. This uncommon shell is found in shallow to moderately shallow water from Florida to the West Indies. under $1-$5

milk moon shell, *Polinices lacteus* Guilding The shell is smooth, glossy, thick and white with a thin yellowish periostracum, It is ½-1½ in. (13-38 mm) high and has a thin, reddish-brown horny operculum. This species is common, found on sand in shallow water from North Carolina to Florida, Gulf of Mexico, and Texas. $1-$3

spotted baby's ear, *Sinum maculatum* Say This shell is is differentiated from the common baby's ear by its more elevated profile and the weak yellowish-brown spots on the white or buff shell. It is about 1½ in. (38 mm) across and has a rudimentary operculum. Uncommon, found in shallow water from North Carolina to Florida and the Gulf of Mexico. $1-$7

common Atlantic baby's ear, *Sinum perspecitivum* Say A very flat shell less than ½ in. (13 mm) high, it is white, 1½ in. (38 mm) in diameter, and the body whorl accounts for more than 75% of the shell. It has a rudimentary operculum, a wide flaring aperture, very thin tan periostracum. It has an extremely large foot; live specimens have the shell virtually surrounded by the animal. Common, in sand in shallow water from Virginia to Florida and to the West Indies. under $1-$2

livid natica

Morocco natica

colorful Atlantic natica

shark's eye

brown moon shell

milk moon shell

spotted baby's ear

common Atlantic baby's ear

Helmet and **Bonnet Shells** (family: *Cassidae*)

The shells in this family are thick, large, colorful, and characterized by having a large parietal shield. The aperture is long, the outer lip is usually thick and has teeth, and the inner lip generally has teeth, ridges or bumps. Members of the genus *Cassis* have a horny, oblong, brown operculum and are used for carving as cameos. The genus *Phalium* has a fan-shaped operculum; in *Cypraecassis,* it is small and oval shaped, or in rare cases absent completely. These species are found on sandy bottoms; the helmets feed on sea urchins and sand dollars.

flame helmet, *Cassis flammea* Linné
The outer shell is yellow with brown marks and streaks, the parietal shield is rounded at the corners, the outer lip has well defined teeth without brown markings between them; inner lip has wrinkles. It reaches a height of 3-6 in. (76-152 mm) and is highly polished. Fairly common, the flame helmet is found in shallow water from the Florida Keys to the West Indies and to Brazil. $4-$6

queen helmet or **emperor helmet,** *Cassis madagascariensis* Lamarck The largest member of the genus, it reaches a height of 14 in. (356 mm). It is white, has a large parietal shield, the outer lip is pale brown or salmon, broad, with elongated teeth and ridges. Teeth on the parietal shield have brownish-black marks between them. Fairly common, on sand in shallow water from southern Florida to the West Indies. $30-$45

king helmet, *Cassis tuberosa* Linné
The tan or yellowish shell is mottled with brown, has brown between the fold on the inner lip and teeth on the outer lip. The parietal shield is triangular and the shell reaches a height of 4-9 in. (102-229 mm). This is the most common Atlantic helmet, found buried in sand in shallow water from North Carolina to the West Indies and Brazil. $12-$50

reticulated cowry helmet, *Cypraecassis testiculus* Linné The large body whorl is brownish to pinkish orange with dark blotches and a criss-cross pattern of lines on the surface. Parietal shield is oval, cream colored with some orange spots; height is 1-3 in. (25-76 mm). Fairly common around reefs in shallow water from southeastern Florida to Texas and to the West Indies and Brazil. $2-$12

Atlantic wood louse, *Morum oniscus* Linné The smallest of the helmet shells, ⅝-1¼ in. (16-32 mm) high, has irregular light-to-dark brown markings or is dark reddish brown overall with white flecks. It has small teeth on the thick outer lip. Common, found under rocks and coral rubble in shallow water below the low-tide line from the Florida Keys to the West Indies and Brazil. $2-$6

smooth Scotch bonnet, *Phalium cicatricosum* Gmelin The pale yellow or white shell is marked with brown spots, similar in coloration to the Scotch bonnet, but the surface is smooth and shiny. It is about 2 in. (51 mm) high and the parietal shield has pimple-like bumps. Fairly common in moderately shallow water in its range from southern Florida to the West Indies and Brazil. $4-$10

Scotch bonnet, *Phalium granulatum* Born The deep spiral grooves on the surface of the shell differentiate this species from the smooth Scotch bonnet. It is 2-4 in. (51-102 mm) high, yellowish or white with pale brown regular spots. The enlarged inner lip has numerous pimple-like bumps. Common, in the sand in shallow water from North Carolina to Florida and to the West Indies, Brazil. $1-$9

royal bonnet, *Sconsia striata* Lamarck The thick grayish shell has brown spots, fine revolving lines and is about 2 in. (51 mm) high. The broad inner lip is polished; the outer lip is thick and has teeth within. Uncommon, it is found in deep water from Florida to the Gulf of Mexico, to the West Indies and Brazil. $17-$24

flame helmet

queen helmet

king helmet

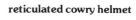

reticulated cowry helmet

Atlantic wood louse

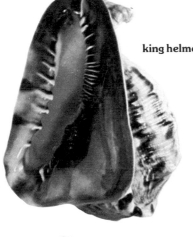

smooth Scotch bonnet

Scotch bonnet

royal bonnet

helmet shells / bonnet shells

Tritons and Distorsios (family: Cymatiidae)

Tritons are large, rugged shells, generally have teeth or folds on both the outer and inner lips of the aperture, and have a long siphonal canal at the base. They have a high spire, a horny thick operculum, and most grow a horny or hairy periostracum which protects the shell. Members of the family are carnivores, feeding on other snails, clams, and starfish, which they anesthesize with a glandular secretion, then insert the proboscis into the helpless prey to feed on the flesh. The large shells have been fashioned into horns since prehistoric times, and Triton, the sea god of mythology, is portrayed with a trumpet made from a large sea shell—thus "Triton's trumpet".

Triton's trumpet, *Charonia variegata* Lamarck   Formerly classified as *Charonia tritonis nobilis.* This strong, solid shell is marked with patches of various colors—tan, brown, red, purple. The aperture is orange, outer lip has pairs of small white teeth; whitish ridges on inner lip. It is 10-15 in. (254-381 mm) high and has a translucent periostracum. Moderately common, found hiding in coral on reefs from southern Florida to the West Indies. $9-$85

The very similar Pacific species, *Charonia tritonis,* Linné, is found in Hawaii and reaches 18 in. (457 mm). $12-$175

dog-head triton, *Cymatium caribbaeum* Clench & Turner   The pale yellow shell is irregularly blotched with gray and white, has heavy revolving ribs, and is 2-3 in. (51-76 mm) high. Common, found in moderately shallow water from Florida to Texas and to the West Indies. $5-$15

angular triton, *Cymatium femorale* Linné Large, up to 7 in. (178 mm) high, the brownish shell is banded in darker shades, has prominent varices with white knobs, and has a white aperture. The periostracum flakes off when the shell is dry. Rare in Florida, but common from the West Indies to Brazil; found in shallow water. $12-$35

Kreb's triton, *Cymatium krebsi* Mörch The white or grayish shell is 2-3 in. (51-76 mm) high. It is not common; its range is from Florida to the West Indies. $3-$10

knobbed triton, *Cymatium muricinum* Röding   Yellowish, grayish white, or brown, the knobbed triton is 1-2 in. (25-51 mm) high, and the whorls may have many dense, beaded spiral cords and axial ribs that can form strong knobs, primarily on the body whorl. The thick outer lip is toothed, yellowish white. Common, found on reefs from southeast Florida to the West Indies, Brazil. $2-$6

gold-mouthed triton, *Cymatium nicobaricum* Röding   Previously classified as *C. chlorostomum,* Lamarck. The grayish or whitish shell is mottled with brown, 2-3 in. (51-76 mm) high, and the surface is divided by crossing horizontal and vertical ribs. The aperture is orange or deep yellow, contrasting brightly with the white teeth. Found around reefs in shallow water, this species is fairly common from southeastern Florida to the West Indies and Brazil. $2-$4

Neopolitan triton, *Cymatium parthenopeum* von Salis   Formerly listed as *C. costatum,* Born. Height is 3-4 in. (76-102 mm), the yellow-brown shell is lightly mottled with darker shades. Live specimens have a hairy periostracum. Aperture is rather large, and the outer lip is thick and knobby. Uncommon, found in moderately shallow water from Florida to the West Indies. $3-$15

Atlantic hairy triton, *Cymatium pileare* Linné   Previously classified as *Cymatium martinianum,* d'Orbigny. Named for the thick, brown, matted, hairy periostracum of the living gastropod, the hairy triton is 3-5 in. (76-127 mm) high, light brown with gray and white bands. Both lips on the aperture are wrinkled with small white teeth on a reddish background. Moderately common, it is found on reefs from South Carolina to Florida and to the West Indies, Brazil, Hawaii. $1-$25

Poulsen's triton, *Cymatium poulseni* Mörch The yellowish-white to brown, well-shouldered shell is 2-3 in. (51-76 mm) high, has a short acute spire, wide aperture. Moderately common, found in deep water from Florida to Texas, West Indies, Venezuela. $2-$8

tiger triton, *Cymatium tigrinus* Broderip Shell is cream colored with brown mottlings, dark "tiger stripes" on both lips, and aperture is edged with light orange. It is 4-7 in. (102-178 mm) high; adults have a flaring outer lip. Rare, found from the Gulf of California to Nicaragua, and in the western Caribbean. $40-$75

dwarf hairy triton, *Cymatium vespaceum* Lamarck   Delicate, small, 1-1½ in. (25-38 mm) high, this shell is yellowish white with brown and white varices. The small aperture is toothed on both lips and the long canal is nearly closed. Uncommon, found in moderately deep water from southern Florida to the West Indies and Brazil. $2-$5

Cymatiidae

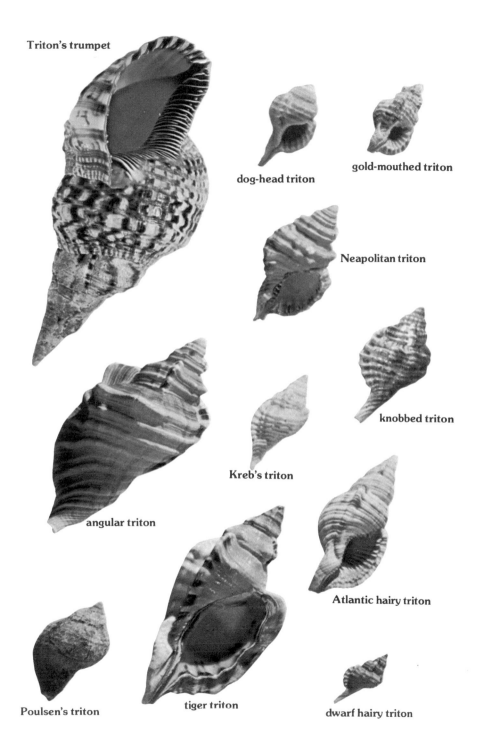

Triton's trumpet

dog-head triton

gold-mouthed triton

Neapolitan triton

angular triton

Kreb's triton

knobbed triton

Atlantic hairy triton

Poulsen's triton

tiger triton

dwarf hairy triton

tritons

Tritons and Distorsios (continued)

Atlantic distorsio, *Distorsio clathrata* Lamarck   This yellowish-white shell is cross-hatched with strong spiral and vertical ribs, is 1-2 in. (25-51 mm) high, and has a hairy periostracum. Aperture is strongly toothed and very distorted; the entire shell has a distorted appearance. Fairly common, it is found in sand in moderately deep water from Florida to the West Indies. $2-$4

Florida distorsio, *Distorsio mcgintyi* Emerson & Puffer   Also considered by some to be *Distorsio constricta mcgintyi,* a subspecies. A tan shell, 1-1½ in. (25-38 mm) high, similar to the Atlantic distorsio but the surface has even coarser crosshatching. It has a hairy periostracum and the outer lip is strongly toothed. Fairly common in moderately deep to deep water from Florida to the West Indies. $4-$8

Frog Shells (family: *Bursidae*)

Frog shells are carnivores, feeding on marine worms and bivalves. They have an oval shaped aperture with a siphonal canal at both the top and the bottom. Members of this family have a horny operculum and a thick outer lip with small teeth.

California frog shell, *Bursa californica* Hinds   Large, 1½-5 in. (38-127 mm) high, it is yellowish white to brown, occasionally with brown spiral lines. The heavy, thick shell has knobbed varices and the aperture is white. Common, in rocks in shallow water from Monterey, Cal. to Baja California. $10-$23

gaudy frog shell, *Bursa corrugata* Perry   An orange-brown shell marked with darker shades, it is 2-3 in. (51-76 mm) high. Outer lip is broad and toothed. Uncommon, found in sand in moderately shallow water from southern Florida to the West Indies. $2-$30

granular frog shell, *Bursa granularis* Röding   Reddish-brown shell blotched with white, 1-2 in. (25-51 mm) high, the yellow aperture has white teeth. Common, found among rocks on reefs from southern Florida to the West Indies. under $1-$4

Tun Shells (family: *Tonnidae*)

Medium- to large-size shells which are light but strong, tuns are carnivores which prey on sea cucumbers and bivalves. The long proboscis can be expanded to engulf the food whole. The shell is nearly round with a greatly enlarged body whorl, has a large aperture with a toothless, thin outer lip, and lacks an operculum.

giant tun, *Tonna galea* Linné   The average shell is about 6 in. (152 mm) high, but this light brown gastropod can attain a height of 10 in. (254 mm). The surface is encircled with grooves, the spire is very low, and the large aperture has a thickened outer lip in mature specimens. Uncommon, tuns are found in sandy, moderately shallow offshore waters from North Carolina to Florida, Gulf of Mexico and Texas, and to the West Indies. $1-$5

Atlantic partridge tun, *Tonna maculosa* Dillwyn   This shell can be pale to warm brown mottled with dark colors and crescent-shaped white marks—giving the surface the appearance of the feathers of a partridge. Shell is thin but strong and has spiral grooves; aperture is tan with a thin sharp outer lip. It is 2-5 in. (51-127 mm) high, fairly common in sand in shallow water near coral reefs from southern Florida to the West Indies, Brazil. $4-$6

Atlantic distorsio

Florida distorsio

California frog shell

gaudy frog shell

granular frog shell

giant tun

Atlantic partridge tun

Murex Shells and Drills (family: *Muricidae*)

There are many genera in this family, found worldwide in tropical and subtropical waters. Extremely variable in appearance, they are characterized by their strong, spiny shells. Typically, murex shells have strong spines and/or varices and a long siphonal canal. Generally found on rocks or reefs in shallow water, members of this family are carnivores—they prey on other snails, bivalves, worms, corals, barnacles, invertebrates. The horny operculum is brown and thick.

Nuttall's hornmouth, *Ceratostoma nuttalli* Conrad Yellowish gray, or brown, often banded in white, it is 1-2 in. (25-51 mm) high. Adults have an apertural tooth. Fairly common in moderately deep water from Monterey, Cal. to Baja California. $3-$18

cabbage murex, *Hexaplex brassica* Lamarck Previously classified as *Murex brassica*. At a height of 8 in. (203 mm), this is our largest member of this genus. It is whitish to pale reddish brown with 3 brown bands. The aperture and edges of the varices are pink. Rather common, found from the Gulf of California to Peru in moderately shallow water. $8-$24

pink-mouthed murex, *Hexaplex erythrostomus* Swainson Formerly listed as *Murex bicolor*, Valenciennes. The rough surface of the shell is chalky white or pinkish white; aperture is shiny, rosy pink; and height is 3-6 in. (76-152 mm). Fairly common, but popular with collectors, it is found in moderately shallow water from the Gulf of California to Peru. $1-$6; white aperture $8-$9

royal murex, *Hexaplex regius* Swainson Aperture lips are bright pink darkening into deep brown on the parietal shield. The surface is mottled brown and the shell reaches 5-6 in. (127-152 mm) high. Fairly common in moderately shallow water from the Gulf of California to Peru. $4-$30

Beau's murex, *Murex beaui* Fisher & Bernardi The spiny varices often have thin wavy webs; the shell is creamy yellow or brownish, has a long canal and is 3-4 in. (76-102 mm) high. Uncommon and a prized collector's piece, found in deep water from southern Florida to Gulf of Mexico and to the West Indies. $5-$70; webbed $85-$120

Bequaert's murex, *Murex bequaerti* Clench & Farfante White, 1-2½ in. (25-63 mm) high, the shell has a sharp apex, a short, closed canal and small aperture. Rare, found in deep water from North Carolina to the Florida Keys and Gulf of Mexico. $25-$40

West Indian murex or **short-frond murex,** *Murex brevifrons* Lamarck A gray shell mottled with white and brown, the fronds on the shoulders curve upwards. It is 3-6 in. (76-

152 mm) high, and the fairly long siphonal canal is partially closed. Fairly common in moderately shallow water from southern Florida and Florida Keys to Gulf of Mexico and to the West Indies. $3-$16

Cabrit's murex, *Murex cabriti* Bernardi The very long siphonal canal has long slender spines which become shorter as they near the tip. The number and size of the spines varies, and they may even be absent. The pinkish-tan shell can reach 3 in. (76 mm) in height. Uncommon, found in moderately deep water from Florida to the Gulf of Mexico and to the West Indies. $10-$45

Caillet's murex, *Murex cailleti* Petit Yellowish with brown bands, this shell is 2-4 in. (50-102 mm) high. The siphonal canal is moderately long, closed and curved; there usually are short spines on the varices. Fairly common in deep water from southern Florida to the West Indies. $7-$10

pitted murex, *Murex cellulosus* Conrad Grayish or tan, the rough shell is about 1 in. (25 mm) high, and the varices at the tip of the closed canal form a "fork". Inside of round aperture is purplish. A shallow water species, common from North Carolina to Gulf of Mexico and to the West Indies. $1-$3

pitted murex, *Murex cellulosus leviculus* Dall Subspecies of previous shell, but not as common, it is found off the eastern coast of Florida to the Gulf of Mexico. $2-$8

gold-mouthed murex, *Murex chrysostoma* Sowerby Tan shell with long siphonal canal, the gold-mouthed murex is 1½-3 in. (36-76 mm) long. Fairly common from Florida to the West Indies. $4-$20

lace murex, *Murex florifer* Reeve A brownish shell with pink apex and aperture, it has a rough surface with broad frond-like spines and is 1-3 in. (25-76 mm) long. Juveniles are usually pink. Common in shallow water from Florida to the West Indies. $4-$50

giant eastern murex, *Murex fulvescens* Sowerby Large, yellowish brown to whitish shell, it has a large body whorl and reaches 7 in. (178 mm) in height. Common, in sandy shallow water where it feeds on the common oyster, from North Carolina to Florida, Texas. $5-$15

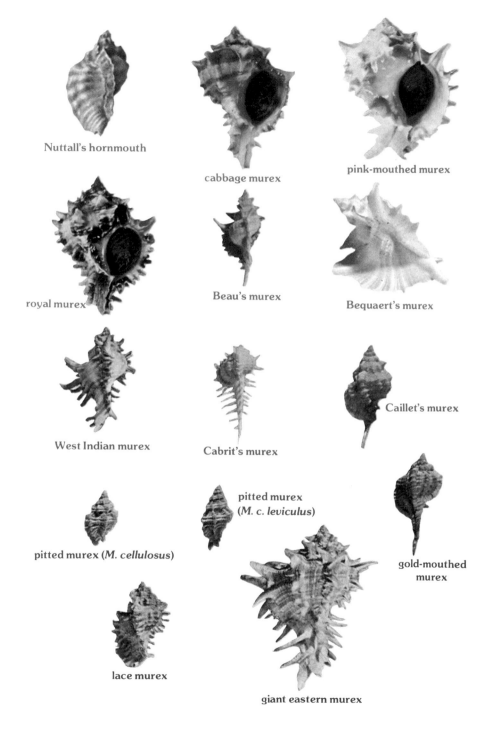

Nuttall's hornmouth

cabbage murex

pink-mouthed murex

royal murex

Beau's murex

Bequaert's murex

West Indian murex

Cabrit's murex

Caillet's murex

pitted murex (*M. cellulosus*)

pitted murex (*M. c. leviculus*)

gold-mouthed murex

lace murex

giant eastern murex

murex shells

Murex Shells (continued)

McGinty's murex, *Murex mcgintyi* M. Smith Grayish white to tan, sometimes with brown markings on varices, the 1 in. (25 mm) high shell has deep revolving ridges across the surface. Siphonal canal is broad, short and partially closed. Rare, it is found in deep water from Florida Keys to the West Indies. $12-$125

apple murex, *Murex pomum* Gmelin This species does not have spines; it is whitish or buff with brown bands and markings. It is 2-4½ in. (51-114 mm) high, the short canal is nearly closed and curves backwards. Common, in shallow water from North Carolina to Florida and to the West Indies, Brazil. under $2-$12

rose murex, *Murex recurvirostris rubidus* Baker Also listed as *Murex rubidus.* Chunky shell, 1½ in. (38 mm) high, it has a long canal which is almost closed, a round aperture and a light yellow operculum. Color varies: cream, pink, orange or red. Common, in shallow water from southern Florida to the West Indies. $4-$20

murex, *Murex recurvirostris sallasi* Abbott & Rehder Also listed as *Murex sallasi.* A cream colored shell with weak brown bands, it has a pointed apex, long siphonal canal and is 1-2 in. (25-51 mm) high. Rare, found in Gulf of Mexico and West Indies. $35

Tryon's murex, *Murex tryoni* Hidalgo This cream colored shell is 1-1½ in. (25-38 mm) high, has a short spire and a long closed canal with spines. Uncommon, in deep water from Florida to the West Indies. $35-$45

Woodring's murex, *Murex woodringi* Clench & Farfante The grayish-white shell occasionally has weak brown markings, is 2-3 in. (51-76 mm) high, and has a pointed apex. The long slender canal is partially closed and the varices have short spines. Uncommon, it is found in deep water from the Gulf of Mexico to the West Indies. $9-$18

black murex, *Muricanthus nigritus* Phillipi Also listed as *Murex nigritus.* A sturdy, solid shell, it reaches a height of 8 in. (152 mm); surface is white with encircling black ribs and spines. Juvenile specimens are almost completely white. Common, found in moderately shallow water in the Gulf of California. $3-$14

Vitularia salebrosa King & Broderip A brownish shell with darker markings, it is solid, 2-3 in. (51-76 mm) high. Surface is rough and there is a row of small knobs at the shoulder. It is common in moderately shallow water from California to Baja California. $1-$5

Drills (family: *Muricidae*)

These small, rock dwellers, drill holes in the shells of bivalves, and most importantly, oysters, which they favor and as a result destroy commericial shellfish beds.

thick-lipped drill, *Eupleura caudata* Say Small solid shell, it varies in color from reddish brown to grayish white, is ½-1 in. (13-25 mm) high, and has a short, almost closed canal. Common, found on oyster beds from Cape Cod, Mass. to Florida. $2-$4

Eupleura muriciformis Broderip A gray shell about 1¼ in. (32 mm) high, it has a thick outer lip and a fairly long, nearly closed canal. Common, in shallow water from the Gulf of California to South America. $1-$3

hexagonal murex, *Muricopsis oxytatus* M. Smith Grayish shell, tinted with pink, it is about 1¼ in. (32 mm) high, the surface is spiny, and the edge of the outer lip has frond-like projections. Uncommon, in moderately shallow water from southern Florida to the West Indies. $3-$8

Muricopsis zeteki Hertlein & Strong Gray shell with brown spines, this species is usually less than 1 in. (25 mm) high, and has a serrated thin outer lip. Common, found in moderately shallow water in Gulf of California. $1-$5

false drill shell, *Pseudoneptunea multangula* Philippi Color varies from cream with brown flecks to, less commonly, brown or orange. The shell is 1-1¼ in. (25-32 mm) high, has a short canal and thin outer lip. Uncommon, found in moderately shallow water from North Carolina to Florida and Texas and to the West Indies. $2-$10

Tampa drill shell, *Urosalpinx tampaensis* Conrad This rugged grayish-brown shell is mottled with white, is ½-1 in. (13-25 mm) high. Destructive to oyster beds, but not as common as *U. cinerea,* Atlantic oyster drill, which is similar but much more numerous and can be devastating to commercial oyster beds. Found in mud flats in western Florida. $1-$2

McGinty's murex

apple murex

rose murex

murex (*M. r. sallasi*)

Tryon's murex

Woodring's murex

black murex

thick-lipped drill

Vitularia salebrosa

Eupleura muriciformis

false drill shell

hexagonal murex *Muricopsis zeteki*

Tampa drill shell

Rock Shells and **Dogwinkles** (family: *Muricidae; also classified in *Thaididae*)

Members of this family are carnivores, have stout shells with a large body whorl, wide aperture, short spire. Most species live on rocks in intertidal areas, though some live in deeper, quiet water; the latter generally have more spines. Live shells exude a green, red, or purple secretion.

wide-mouthed rock shell, *Purpura patula* Linné A large body whorl makes up most of the rough, solid shell in this species which is 2-3½ in. (51-89 mm) high. The surface is grayish green or brown with prominent nodules in young specimens; interior is salmon colored. Common, in intertidal waters on rocks from Florida to the West Indies. $1-$3

deltoid rock shell, *Thais deltoidea* Lamarck Stocky gray or white shell with brown and violet blotches, it has three spiral rows of knobs on the body whorl, with the two rows on the shoulders forming blunt spines; 1-2 in. (25-51 mm) high, It is common, found among rocks, often heavily encrusted, in intertidal areas from Florida to the West Indies. $1-$3

Florida rock shell, *Thais haemastoma floridana* Conrad Cream or orange shell with brown marks, it is 2-3 in. (51-76 mm) high, has a thick outer lip, short canal and flesh-colored aperture. Common, found in intertidal areas on oyster beds from North Carolina to Florida and Gulf of Mexico, and to the West Indies and Brazil. $1-$4

channeled dogwinkle, *Nucella canaliculata* Duclos Also listed as *Thais canaliculata.* White or grayish to brown, the shell has a prominent spire, deep suture, and is 1-1½ in. (25-38 mm) high. Common, found in rock crevices in intertidal areas from Alaska to Monterey, Cal. $1-$3

frilled dogwinkle, *Nucella lamellosa* Gmelin Also listed as *Thais lamellosa.* Form and color of the shell is variable: white to light brown, occasionally with brown bands, smooth or sculptured. It is 1-3¼ in. (25-83 mm) high, outer lip is white and broadly flared. Common, in protected rock crevices in intertidal area to below the low-tide line from Alaska to California. $2-$8

Coral Shells (family: *Magilidae;* also classified in *Coralliophilidae*)

Small, thick shells, they may be sculptured with spiral series of spines or be smooth; they can be white, yellow, or pink and in some cases have a bright purple aperture. Coral shells are carnivores, and live with stony and soft corals, and a few species among anemones.

short coral shell, *Coralliophil a abbreviata* Lamarck White to grayish-white, thick shell with a large body whorl and low spire, it has a deep canal which is open and the outer lip is strongly toothed. It is about 1 in. (25 mm) high, and aperture is pink or violet. Common, at bases of stony corals and sea fans from Florida to the West Indies, Brazil. $2-$6

Coralliophila costata Blainville Gray with a purple aperture, this sturdy shell is about 1 in. (25 mm) high, and the outer lip is somewhat thickened. Fairly common on coral from Gulf of California to Panama. $6-$7

Coralliophila deburghiae Reeve Light gray to tan, sculptured surface with knobs at sutures, it is 1-1½ in. (25-38 mm) high. Uncommon, found on corals in Florida and the Gulf of Mexico. $10

Dove Shells (family: *Columbellidae*)

Small shells, members of this family can be ovate to elongate in shape, smooth or sculptured, and have high pointed or low broad spires. They feed on algae.

common dove shell, *Columbella mercatoria* Linné Extremely variable in color, the shell is usually white with brown, but may be solid white, or spotted with yellow or orange. The solid shell is only ½ in. (13 mm) high, and has many revolving grooves. Common in shallow water from Florida to West Indies. $1-$2

Nassas and **Dog Whelks** (family: *Nassariidae*)

Small carnivorous snails, most species are scavengers, but some prey on oysters and thin-shelled mollusks. Surface may be smooth or heavily sculptured, spire is pointed, and the short canal is open.

variable nassa, *Nassarius consensus* Ravenel About ½ in. (13 mm) high, the shell is light brown with white markings. Common, found in shallow water from Florida to the West Indies.   under $1

channeled dog whelk, *Nassarius fossatus* Gould Up to 1¾ in. (45 mm) high, this is the largest west coast member of the species. It is a shiny yellowish-tan shell with a bright orange interior, a high spire and fine spiral lines. Common, in shallow water from British Columbia to Baja California. $2-$7

Nassarius hotessieri, d'Orbigny Small, ½-1 in. (6-13 mm) high, the gray shell has axial ribs along each whorl. Common, in shallow water in Florida and Gulf of Mexico. $1-$3

wide-mouthed rock shell

deltoid rock shell

Florida rock shell

channeled dogwinkle

frilled dogwinkle

short coral shell

Coralliophila costata

Coralliophila deburghiae

common dove shell

variable nassa

channeled dog whelk

Nassarius hotessieri

rock shells / dogwinkles / coral shells / dove shells / nassas / dog whelks

Small Whelks, Cantharus Shells, Dwarf Tritons and **Pisa Shell** (family: *Buccinum*)

Members of this family are carnivores; they are scavengers and also actively prey on bivalves by means of a long proboscis. All species have a well defined canal and horny operculum. The surface of the shell may be smooth or have spiral or axial sculpture or a combination.

common northern whelk, *Buccinum undatum* Linné Yellowish white to yellow-brown, live specimens have a light brown periostracum; surface has numerous weak spiral cords. It is 3-4 in. (76-102 mm) high, very common on rocks in shallow to moderately deep water from the Arctic Ocean to New Jersey and also to Europe. This snail is eaten in some parts of Europe. $3-$12

gaudy cantharus, *Cantharus auritula* Link A stout solid shell, ¾-1¼ in. (19-32 mm) high, it is mottled with brown, gray, black, has a short canal and thick outer lip. Common, found in shallow water from southern Florida to the West Indies. $1-$2

cancellate cantharus, *Cantharus cancellaria* Conrad A reddish-brown shell marked with white mottlings and sculptured both spirally and axially, it is ¾-1¼ in. (19-32 mm) high, elongated, with a thick outer lip. It is common, in shallow water from Florida to Texas. under $1-$5

Cantharus ringens Reeve Grayish-brown shell, surface is sculptured with prominent spiral cords. About 1 in. (25 mm) high, toothed outer lip is thickened. Common from Gulf of California to Central America. $2-$3

tinted cantharus, *Cantharus tinctus* Conrad A solid shell about 1 in. (25 mm) high, color is variable, it has a very short canal, thick outer lip, and a tooth at the upper end of the aperture. Common, found in weeds in intertidal zone

from North Carolina to Florida and Texas and to the West Indies. $1-$2

arrow dwarf triton, *Colubraria lanceolata* Menke A slender gray shell with orange-brown blotches, the surface has many fine vertical lines. About 1 in. (25 mm) high, it is common, found under rocks in shallow to moderately deep water from North Carolina to Florida and the West Indies. $3-$8

Colubraria testacea Mörch Primarily brown, but with lighter bands, the shell is ½-1½ in. (13-38 mm) high and the surface has fine lines of spiral cords. Uncommon, found from Florida to the West Indies. $5-$12

New England neptune or **ten-ridged whelk,** *Neptunea decemcostata* Say This shell is gray with prominent reddish-brown ridges and white aperture, and is 3-4 in. (76-102 mm) high. A common species, but it is not generally found in good condition on shore. They are frequently caught in fishermen's nets and lobster traps. Found on rocky bottoms in moderately shallow water from Nova Scotia to Massachusetts. $4-$20

pisa shell, *Pisania pusio* Linné This smooth polished shell is purplish brown, marked with irregular dark and light spots, and is about 1½ in. (38 mm) high. Spire is well developed and the apex is pointed. Common, in moderately shallow water and on reefs from southern Florida to West Indies. $1-$3

gaudy cantharus

cancellate cantharus

common northern whelk

Cantharus ringens

tinte cantharus

arrow dwarf triton

Colubraria testacea

New England neptune

pisa shell

small whelks / cantharus shells / dwarf tritons / pisa shell

Whelks and Crown Conchs (family: *Melongenidae*)

Moderately large to large, shallow-water species, the members of this family have a solid shell, large body whorl, and a horny oval operculum which is pointed at one end. They are primarily carnivores, either scavengers or they prey on live tulip snails and oysters. Shell sculpture is varied.

channeled whelk, *Busycon canaliculatum* Linné This pear-shaped shell is 3½-7½ in. (89-190 mm) high, has a broad, deeply channeled suture and a large yellow-brown aperture. The shell is gray to cream colored, covered with a thick hairy gray periostracum. Common, it is found in sand and mud in intertidal zone to just below low-tide line from Massachusetts to northern Florida; also introduced in California. As late as 1925 this species was sold as food in Boston. $2-$5

Kiener's whelk, *Busycon carica eliceans* Montfort A heavy shell with strong spines on a large body whorl, it is 4-9 in. (102-229 mm) high, and has a long open canal. The surface is grayish white to grayish brown and the aperture is reddish orange. Very similar to the knobbed whelk, *B. carica,* Gmelin, except Kiener's whelk is heavier, has heavier spines on the body whorl and has a spiral swelling around the lower part of the body whorl. Kiener's whelk is common, found in shallow water from North Carolina to Florida. $5-$6

The knobbed whelk is also common in shallow water, but its range extends from Massachusetts to Florida. $3-$8

turnip whelk, *Busycon coarctatum* Sowerby This species has a long open canal, a short spire with the sutures bearing short, brown, sharp spines. The grayish surface is streaked vertically with brownish-purple marks, aperture is yellow-orange, and it may attain a height of 6 in. (152 mm). Uncommon, found in moderately shallow water in the Gulf of Mexico. $10-$20

lightning whelk, *Busycon contrarium* Conrad A large tan to grayish-white shell, it is 2½-16 in. (64-406 mm) high, and has fine reddish-brown axial lines on the surface. This is a sinistral shell (rarely, dextral) with a large body whorl which narrows to a long open canal; aperture is white. Common in sand from low-tide line to shallow water, it is found from North Carolina to Florida and Texas. $1-$15; right-handed $120

pear whelk, *Busycon spiratum* Lamarck Previously classified as *B. pyrum,* Dillwyn. This pear-shaped shell usually has smooth, rounded shoulders and a long siphonal canal. It is flesh colored, streaked with reddish brown and is 3-5 in. (76-127 mm) high. The tan periostracum is fuzzy. Common, in shallow water from North Carolina to Florida and the Gulf states. $4-$5

Florida crown conch, *Melongena corona* Gmelin This brown shell is banded with white, blue and yellow, is 1-8 in. (25-203 mm) high, and has a claw-like operculum. The presence of spines varies greatly with some forms being spineless (as a result of dietary deficiency), others with one or more rows of spines on the shoulders, and still others, rarely, are multi-spined. It is primarily a scavenger but will attack live bivalves. Common, on mud or muddy sand in shallow water from Florida to Gulf of Mexico, Alabama, to Mexico. under $1-$3

West Indian crown conch or **brown crown conch,** *Melongena melongena* Linné Whitish with brownish-purple bands which in some specimens cover most of the shell, it is 2-7 in. (51-178 mm) high, has a short spire with vertical ribs. Body whorl may be smooth or have 2 or 3 rows of sharp spines on periphery, and a row of spines near the base. It feeds on mollusks, primarily bivalves, including oysters. It is found in mud and sand in brackish water at mouths of bays or lagoons in the West Indies. $4-$15

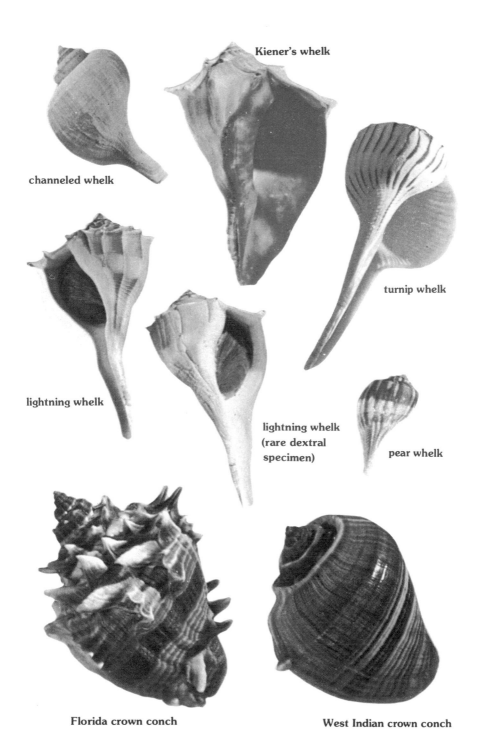

Kiener's whelk

channeled whelk

turnip whelk

lightning whelk

lightning whelk
(rare dextral
specimen)

pear whelk

Florida crown conch

West Indian crown conch

whelks / crown conchs

Tulip Shells, Horse Conch, and **Spindle Shells** (family: *Fasciolariidae*)

These snails are spindle shaped, have a strong thick shell, elongated spire and rather long siphonal canal. The horny operculum is oval shaped and completely covers the opening when the animal is withdrawn. They are predators with slow, deliberate movement, feeding on mollusks, and in some cases, sea worms and barnacles.

Branham's tulip, *Fasciolaria branhamae* Rehder & Abbott   This shell is also listed as subspecies, *Fasciolaria hunteria branhamae.* It is 3-5 in. (76-127 mm) high, which is larger than *F. hunteria,* and it also has a longer siphonal canal. The shell is whitish with brown-colored spiral lines. Fairly common, but in deep water in Gulf of Mexico. $2-$10

banded tulip, *Fasciolaria hunteria*   Perry A tan shell with narrow brown spiral lines, one color variation has bluish-gray vertical cloudings, the other has similar orange markings. It is 2-4 in. (51-102 mm) high, and the surface is smooth. A common species, found in shallow water in sandy mud and weeds from North Carolina to Florida and the Gulf of Mexico. under $1-$3

true tulip, *Fasciolaria tulipa*   Linné   The color of this shell is variable—usually grayish green or grayish white with brownish or orange axial splotches. It is 2-9 in. (51-229 mm) high, and preys on other gastropods and bivalves, but favors large snails such as pear whelks, banded tulips and small queen conchs. Common, found on sand and mud in intertidal zone to moderately shallow water from North Carolina to Florida, Texas and to the West Indies. $2-$15

short-tailed latirus, *Latirus brevicaudatus* Reeve   The knobby whorls of this shell have well defined sutures, it is light brown with darker encircling lines and is 1-2 in. (25-51 mm) high. Moderately common, found in shallow water in the Florida Keys and West Indies. $2-$6

brown-lined latirus, *Latirus infundibulum* Gmelin   This elongated tan shell has many orange-brown spiral cords, is about 2 in. (51 mm) high, has a narrow, long canal and 2 or 3 pleats on the inner lip. It is found in moderately shallow water from southern Florida (uncommon) to the West Indies. $3-$15

McGinty's latirus, *Latirus mcgintyi*   Pilsbry A heavy, solid yellowish shell, it has brown markings between strong, rounded vertical ribs and is ½-2½ in. (13-63 mm) high. Uncommon, it is found in moderately shallow water near reefs in southern Florida. $2-$8

chestnut latirus, *Leucozonia nassa*   Gmelin A heavy chestnut-brown shell, it has 9-10 pronounced knobs on shoulders of the lower whorls, a short open canal and is 1-2 in. (25-51 mm) high. A common species, it is found under rocks or wet sand on reefs from the intertidal zone to below the low-tide line. Its range is from Florida to Texas and to the West Indies. $1-$3

white-spotted latirus, *Leucozonia ocellata* Gmelin   A small, 1 in. (25 mm), heavy brown shell, it has whitish knobs at the periphery of the whorls and small white spots at the base of the shell. The apex is white in mature specimens. Common, found in the intertidal area from Florida to the West Indies. $2-$5

Opeatostoma pseudodon   Burrow   The surface of this grayish white shell has dark brown revolving lines. The base of the aperture has a long needle-like tooth and the shell is 2½ in. (63 mm) high. Common, in moderately shallow water from Gulf of California to Peru. $2-$6

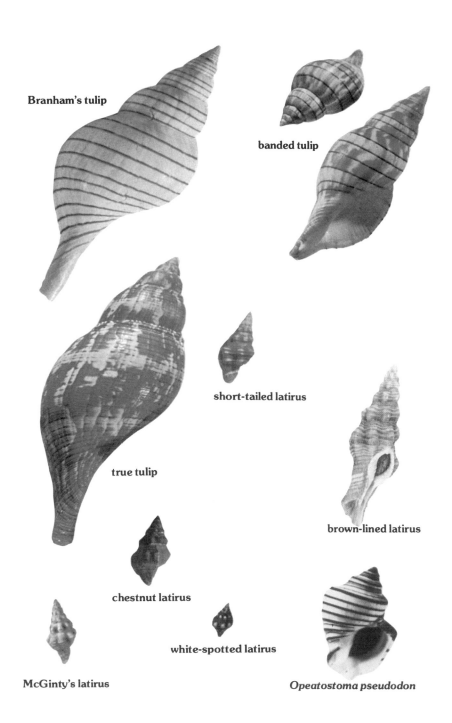

Branham's tulip

banded tulip

short-tailed latirus

true tulip

brown-lined latirus

chestnut latirus

white-spotted latirus

McGinty's latirus

Opeatostoma pseudodon

tulip shells

Horse Conchs and Spindles

Florida horse conch, *Pleuroploca gigantea* Kiener This very large, heavy shell can reach 24 in. (610 mm) in height. The immature specimens are orange; older shells are grayish white to salmon and brown with a brown flaky periostracum; and rarely, some are albinos. The whorls on the spire have triangular knobs, and the long, open canal is slightly twisted. The horse conch is one of the largest gastropods in the world. It feeds primarily on other large snails—tulip shells, lightning whelks, lace murex—and on pen shells. The horse conch prevents its prey from closing the aperture by holding the victim's operculum and then inserts its proboscis and eats the soft parts of the animal. This is a common species, but large shells are becoming rare due to overcollecting. It is found in sand and mud from the low-tide line to moderately shallow water, from North Carolina to Florida, Texas, and Mexico. large $35-$75; large albino $200

Pleuroploca reevei Philippi Similar to the Florida horse conch, except *P. reevei* does not have knobs on the spire whorls. Large, 8-18 in. (203-457 mm) high; some regard this shell as merely another knob-less form of the Florida horse conch. Range limited to Florida. $2-$15

Coue's spindle, *Fusinus couei* Petit A white, tall shell of 4 in. (102 mm), it has distinct sutures, a small aperture, and a long canal which is nearly closed. Common, found in deep water in the Gulf of Mexico. $2-$4

Fusinus dupetitthouarsi Kiener White or cream colored, the shell has a greenish-yellow periostracum, is 6-10 in. (152-254 mm) high, and the open canal is very long. Common, in moderately shallow water in the Gulf of California. $3-$22

ornamented spindle, *Fusinus eucosmius* Dall The color of this shell can vary from pure white to orange-white; periostracum is thick, yellowish. Spire is sharply pointed, canal is long and thin and the shell is 2½ in. (64 mm) high. Fairly common in moderately deep water in the Gulf of Mexico. $4-$10

Fusinus halistrepus Dall A slender white shell, it is 1½ in. (38 mm) long. Uncommon, it is found in the Gulf of Mexico. $8-$12

Fusinus helenae Bartsch An elongated white shell, it is 1½ in. (38 mm) long and has a long canal. Uncommon, it is found in the Gulf of Mexico. $7-$20

turnip spindle, *Fusinus timessus* Dall Rather chunky shell, 3 in. (76 mm) high, it has a deep suture and a long, nearly-closed canal. Shell is white, occasionally tinted with yellow-orange. Uncommon, found in deep water in the Gulf of Mexico. $3-$10

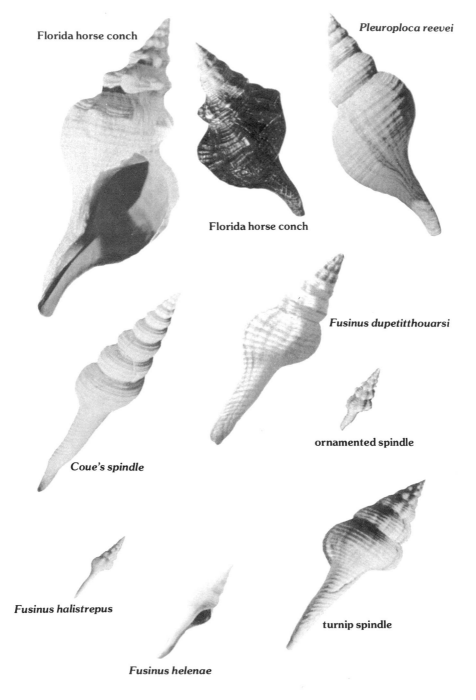

Florida horse conch

Pleuroploca reevei

Florida horse conch

Fusinus dupetitthouarsi

ornamented spindle

Coue's spindle

Fusinus halistrepus

Fusinus helenae

turnip spindle

Olive Shells (family: *Olividae*)

These elongated cylindrical shells are smooth and glossy because the mantle and foot in the living snail usually covers and protects the shell. They have a large body whorl and small conical spire. Those in the genus *Oliva* usually lack an operculum while other genera may have them. They are carnivores, preying on bivalves and crabs which they enclose in the foot and then burrow into the sand to digest the catch.

Caribbean olive, *Oliva caribaeensis* Dall & Simpson This shell is generally a grayish purple with purplish aperture, but some varieties are reddish brown with a light aperture. The shiny smooth surface also has darker lines and white specks. It is 1½ in. (38 mm) high, and is common in the intertidal zone in the West Indies. $2-$3

Oliva incrassata Lightfoot Solid shell of about 2 in. (51 mm) high, it has a wider aperture than most olives, and the pinkish-gray surface is flecked and streaked with lavender and gray. The inner lip is bright pink in fresh specimens. Common, except for an occasional rare yellow unmarked specimen, it is found from the Gulf of California to Peru. $2-$13; corded $40-$50

tent olive, *Oliva porphyria* Linné The largest of our olives, this 4 in. (102 mm) shell is grayish with a network of thin brown zigzag lines, which in some areas are dense enough to form brown patches. Fairly common, it is found in shallow water in the Gulf of California. Rare specimens are corded. $10-$100

netted olive, *Oliva reticularis* Lamarck White or gray shell, the shiny surface is marked with a pattern of purplish-brown net-like lines. Common species, 1½-2 in. (38-51 mm) high, it is found in sand in shallow to moderately shallow water from southern Florida to the West Indies. $1-$5

Oliva reticularis bollingi Clench Subspecies of netted olive, it is 1½-2 in. (38-51 mm) high. Cream colored with indistinct markings, it is moderately common in sand in deep water from southern Florida to the Bahamas. $2-$4

Oliva reticularis greenwayi Clench This is another subspecies, marked with dark reddish-brown bands, and found in southern Florida and the Bahamas. Moderately common, 1½-2 in. (38-51 mm) high, found in sand. $2-$4

Oliva reticularis olorinella Duclos The color of this subspecies varies from bluish gray to grayish, and a rare specimen, albino. Common, except for albino, 1½-2 in. (38-51 mm) high, found in Bahamas and throughout the West Indies. $3-$5

lettered olive, *Oliva sayana* Ravenel This strong shell is highly polished, is cream to gray with the surface heavily marked in reddish brown zigzag markings, and is 2-2¾ in. (51-70 mm) high. Common species, usually found buried in sand with only the siphon sticking out. Its range is North Carolina to Florida and Texas, and to the West Indies, Brazil. under $1-$10

purple dwarf olive, *Olivella biplicata* Sowerby A grayish shell (sometimes almost white), it has a purplish band at the base and the outer lip is purplish within. Immature and young specimens are tinted with purple. Common species, ½-1 in. (13-38 mm) high, it is found on sand from the intertidal zone to moderately deep water from Vancouver Island, B.C. to Baja California. under $1-$2

West Indian dwarf olive, *Olivella nivea* Gmelin Small, ½-1 in. (13-25 mm) high, the shiny surface is white with orange-brown markings. Common, found in the intertidal zone to moderately deep water from Florida to the West Indies. $1-$3

Caribbean olive   *Oliva incrassata*

tent olive

netted olive   *Oliva reticularis bollingi*

Oliva reticularis greenwayi

Oliva reticularis olorinella

lettered olive

purple dwarf olive

West Indian dwarf olive

olive shells

61

Miter Shells (family: *Mitridae*)

The shape of these shells varies from ovate to elongate, the surface usually has spiral cords, and in some cases may have axial ribs or be smooth without any sculpture. They are found in sand or coral rubble, where these carnivores feed, by means of a long proboscis, on marine worms and occasionally mollusks. The operculum is absent, but they have a thin periostracum, and a sharply pointed spire.

Barbados miter, *Mitra barbadensis* Gmelin
The elongated shell is tan with white marks, the surface has week spiral cords, and the aperture is long and narrow. This common shell is 1-1½ in. (25-38 mm) high and is found in intertidal areas around open oceanic reefs from southern Florida to the West Indies. under $1-$6

royal Florida miter, *Mitra florida* Gould
The smooth white shell has many spiral rows of yellowish-brown dots and is 1½-2 in. (38-51 mm) high. Rare, found in moderately shallow water on sand around coral reefs from southern Florida to the West Indies. $15-$50

Chank Shells (family: *Xancidae;* also classified in *Turbinellidae*)

Members of this family range in size from ¼-14 in. (13-356 mm) high, have a fairly long siphonal canal and are carnivores. They are found in tropical and subtropical water from just below the low-tide line to very deep water.

chank shell or **lamp shell,** *Xancus angulatus* Lightfoot   Previously classified as *Turbinella scolymus,* Gmelin; also classified as *Turbinella angulata,* Lightfoot. This yellowish-white shell is heavy and has prominent knobs on the shoulders. It is 5-14 in. (127-356 mm) high, has a rounded apex, a horny claw-like operculum, and a brown periostracum. This carnivorous species feeds on tube worms and bivalves. Uncommon, found in shallow water on sand or rubble from southern Florida to the West Indies. $5-$8; over 15 in. (400 mm) $35-$50

Vase Shells (family: *Vasidae*)

Representatives of this family can be heavy top-shaped or elongated ovate with a narrow base; or spindle-shaped with a long slender canal. They are found in sand near reefs; are carnivores, feeding on bivalves and sea worms. Operculum is clawlike and they usually have a heavy periostracum.

spiny vase shell, *Vasum capitellus* Linné
This vase-shaped yellowish-brown shell is 2-3 in. (51-76 mm) high, and the surface has strongly rounded vertical ribs which produce heavy spines on the shoulders. The base of the body whorl has two rows of spines. Fairly common in shallow water in the West Indies. $2-$3

Caribbean vase shell, *Vasum muricatum* Born   This large, heavy vase-shaped shell is 2½-5 in. (64-127 mm) high, yellowish white in color, covered with a brown periostracum. The last spire whorls have strongly angled knobs at the periphery, the wide body whorl has 9-10 strong triangular-shaped knobs at the periphery, often with smaller knobs below, and there are 2-4 rows of triangular knobs on the ridges near the base. Fairly common in shallow water from southern Florida to the West Indies. $1-$3

Harp Shells (family: *Harpidae*)

This family is characterized by the large flaring apertures and vertical ribbing. The shells are ornate, have no operculum and are primarily Indo-Pacific, with but a single species found off North America.

harp shell, *Harpa crenata* Swainson
A pale shell with purplish-brown ribs and spots on the ribs, it has brown and violet chevron-like marks in the spaces between the ribs. Most of the shell consists of the enlarged body whorl; spire is short, pointed; aperture flares; and the shell is 2-3 in. (51-76 mm) high. It is fairly common, found in moderately shallow water in the Gulf of California. $3-$8

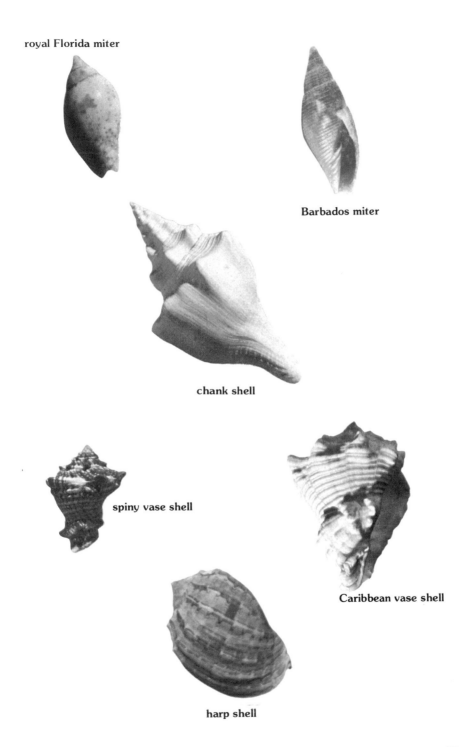

royal Florida miter

Barbados miter

chank shell

spiny vase shell

Caribbean vase shell

harp shell

miter shells / chank shell / vase shells / harp shell

Volutes (family: *Volutidae*)

The shells in this family are among the most costly specimens to buy. These colorful prized shells are elongated to broadly oval, and most volutes have a bulbous nuclear whorl at the apex. Adults are generally smooth, but they can occasionally have spines or knobs near the upper part of the body whorl. Volutes may or may not have an operculum. They are carnivores and feed on small marine invertebrates.

Scaphella cuba Clench   Also listed as *Voluta cuba*. Cream or white with spiral rows of reddish-brown spots, this rare species reaches a height of 2 in. (51 mm). Its range includes the north coast of Cuba and the Florida Straits. $60

Dohrn's volute, *Scaphella dohrni* Sowerby Also listed as *Voluta dohrni*. This slender gray or white shell is marked with spiral rows of squarish brown spots, has a moderately tall spire and is 2-4 in. (51-102 mm) high. Rare, found in deep water off the southern half of Florida. $20-$50

dubious volute, *Scaphella dubia* Broderip Also listed as *Voluta dubia*. A slender shell, tan to pinkish with brown spots, but the markings are fewer than on Dohrn's volute. It is 3-4 in. (76-102 mm) high and there are vertical ribs on the upper whorls. Uncommon, found in deep water off southern Florida and in the Gulf of Mexico. $25

Scaphella georgiana Clench   Also listed as *Voluta georgiana*. This tan shell reaches a height of 3-4 in. (76-102 mm). The brown spots on the surface are less dense and smaller than in the other spotted volutes. This is a rare species, found from Georgia to the east coast of Florida. $30-$50

Gould's volute, *Scaphella gouldiana* Dall Also listed as *Voluta gouldiana*. This yellowish-gray shell may have broad brown spiral bands or occasionally it may be mostly white. Surface is sculptured with short ribs at the shoulders; it reaches 2-3 in. (51-76 mm) in height. Uncommon, found in deep water from North Carolina to Florida and the West Indies. $20-$40

junonia, *Scaphella junonia* Shaw   This rather large shell, 3-6 in. (76-152 mm) high, is creamy white with rows of squarish spots which are dark brown or reddish orange. Very popular with collectors but not as rare as it once was believed to be, since it is found by shrimp fishermen regularly. There is no operculum. Uncommon, found in moderately deep water from North Carolina to Florida and Gulf of Mexico. $5-$50

Kiener's volute, *Scaphella kieneri* Clench Also listed as *Voluta kieneri* and *Auriniopsis kieneri*. This large slender shell is tan and has rectangular-shaped spots which are dark brown or black in spiral rows around the shell. The shell is 5-8 in. (127-203 mm) high, and while considered rare at one time, it has become more available as a by-product of the shrimp fishing industry. Fairly common, in deep water in the Gulf of Mexico. $15-$60

music volute, *Voluta musica*   Linné A grayish-white or pinkish shell, it is marked with spots and lines resembling the staff and notes of musical notation. It is thick shelled, oval shaped, 2-3½ in. (51-89 mm) high and has a small horny operculum. Fairly common, it is found in coral sand in shallow water in the West Indies. $7-$35

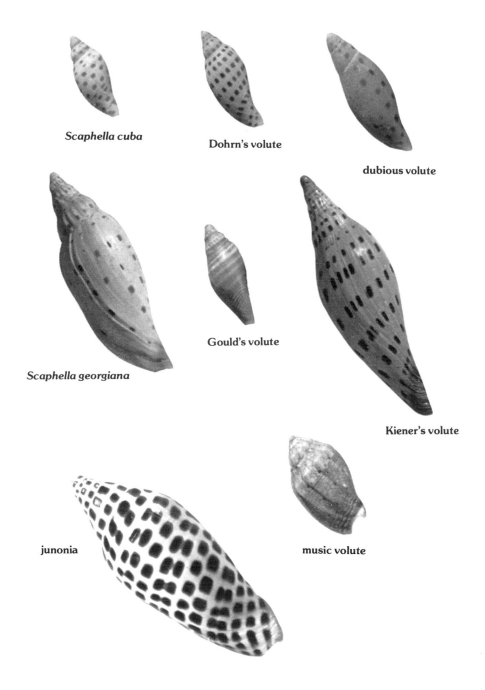

Scaphella cuba

Dohrn's volute

dubious volute

Scaphella georgiana

Gould's volute

Kiener's volute

junonia

music volute

Nutmegs (family: Cancellariidae)

These oval-shaped shells have a broad aperture ending in a short canal, are both spirally and axially sculptured. They lack an operculum but they can seal the shell opening with a mixture of sand and mucus. Nutmegs are carnivores and can be found in both shallow and fairly deep water.

nutmeg, Cancellaria conradiana Dall Most macologists believe this shell is really only a variation of the common nutmeg, C. reticulata. It is 1-1½ in. (25-38 mm) high, oval shaped but elongated slightly, has brownish-orange bands on a white shell. The shell is sculptured in both directions. Common in shallow water from North Carolina to both coasts of Florida. under $1-$3

common nutmeg, Cancellaria reticulata Linné Broader and more heavily colored than C. conradiana, this shell is 1-1½ in. (25-38 mm) high, is cream or gray with orange-brown bands. The sculpture consists of both spiral cords and weak axial ribs. Common in sand in shallow water from North Carolina to Florida and Texas. $2-$5

Adele's nutmeg, Cancellaria reticulata adelae Pilsbry This subspecies of the common nutmeg is 1-1½ in. (25-38 mm) high, has a cream colored shell marked with orange-brown bands, and the body whorl is smooth. This snail is rare, found in shallow water in the Florida Keys. $2-$4

Philippi's nutmeg, Trigonostoma tenerum Philippi About 1 in. (25 mm) high, this thin shell has four whorls, broad shoulders and blunt beads covering the surface. It is pale yellow-orange. Not common, found in moderately shallow water from southern Florida to the West Indies. $6-$7

Marginellas (family: Marginellidae)

Margin shells, as they are also called, are small, shiny, usually colorful shells, and most have a low spire. They have no operculum, aperture is narrow and the outer lip has a thick margin, thus the common name. These snails have a large foot and mantle, the latter often covering most of the shell. They are carnivores and live in sand on reefs amid marine growth or under rocks.

common Atlantic margin shell, Prunum apicinum Menke This shell is solid, ½ in. (13 mm) high, has a low spire and an enlarged body whorl. The glossy surface is usually bright yellow to brownish orange, but a gray variety is found in the Florida Keys. There are 2 or 3 brownish spots on the outer lip. Rare specimens are sinistral. This is a very common shell, found in shallow water from North Carolina to Florida and the Gulf of Mexico and to the West Indies. under $1-$2; sinistral $25

orange marginella, Prunum carneum Storer The shiny orange body whorl of this shell has white bands. It is ¾ in. (19 mm) high and has a thickened, rolled outer lip. Not common, it is found on coral reefs from below the low-tide line to moderately shallow water. $3-$20

white-spotted marginella, Prunum guttatum Dillwyn The shiny cream colored shell has three pinkish-gray bands on the body whorl and is covered with irregular white flecks. The outer lip is smooth white with brown spots. It is ¾ in. (19 mm) high, fairly common, found in shallow water in coral sand from southern Florida to the West Indies. $1-$4

nutmeg

common nutmeg

Philippi's nutmeg

Adele's nutmeg

common Atlantic margin shell

orange marginella

white-spotted marginella

Cone Shells (family: *Conidae*)

These shells are easily recognizable by their conic shape, which the common name describes. They are generally solid and have vividly colored shells decorated in a great variety of patterns. They are among the favorites of shell collectors and some specimens sell for thousands of dollars. The spire varies from flattened to elevated; the surface can be smooth or have cords; the operculum is horny and elongated, but only one-fifth the length

(continued on page 70)

Austin's cone, *Conus austini* Rehder & Abbott   The whitish shell is 1-2½ in. (25-64 mm) high, has a surface sculpture of spiral cords crossing weak vertical lines. It has a high spire with a pointed apex. Found in moderately deep water from the Florida Keys to the West Indies, it was once considered fairly rare but is now often found by shrimp fishermen. $10-$20

California cone, *Conus californicus* Reeve This yellowish-brown shell is covered by a reddish-brown periostracum, has a low spire and is ¾-1½ in. (19-38 mm) high. This cone preys on a great variety of other living gastropods. It is fairly common, found in sand and gravel from low-tide line to moderately deep water from San Francisco, California to southern Baja California. $1-$6

Clark's cone, *Conus clarki* Rehder & Abbott A whitish shell, it is 1-1½ in. (25-38 mm) high, similar to *C. austini,* but Clark's cone has strongly beaded cords at the shoulders. Found in moderately deep water in the Gulf of Mexico; rare. $225

carrot cone, *Conus daucus* Hwass The color of this solid shell varies from dark orange to bright yellow with some specimens having a light yellowish central band. It is 1-2 in. (25-51 mm) high and the spire is usually marked with white blotches on the orange background. Not common, found in moderately deep water from Florida to the West Indies. $5-$75

Florida cone, *Conus floridanus* Gabb The color of this shell is variable, usually white with broad patches of orange or yellow and a white band on the body whorl. It is 1½-1¾ in. (38-44 mm) high with an elevated spire, sharp apex and distinct suture. Common, found on sand from the low-tide line to moderately shallow water from North Carolina to both coasts of Florida. $5-$12

dark Florida cone, *Conus floridanus floridensis* Sowerby This cone is 1½-1¾ in. (38-44 mm) high, similar to *C. floridanus* but darker and with dominant rows of brown dots. Moderately common, found on sand from the low-tide line to moderately shallow water from North Carolina to both coasts of Florida. $4-$6

Burry's cone, *Conus floridanus burryae* Clench   The body whorl of this subspecies is brown, spire is light with brown lines on whorls. It is 1½-1¾ in. (38-44 mm) high, uncommon, in fairly shallow water in the Florida Keys. $20

glory-of-the-Atlantic cone, *Conus granulatus* Linné   The shoulders of this shell are rounded so that the spire lacks the pointiness of most cones. It is 1-1¾ in. (25-44 mm) high, the surface is marked with distinct spiral lines, color variable from orange to pink with spiral brown markings and a band around the middle of the body whorl. Rare, found on reefs in moderately deep water from the Florida Keys to the West Indies. $100-$525

Jasper cone, *Conus jaspideus* Gmelin This gray shell has evenly spaced spiral cords with rows of brown and white dots and a rather high pointed spire. It is ½-¾ in. (13-19 mm) high, very common, found in sand in shallow water from North Carolina to Florida and the West Indies and to Brazil. $6-$7

Julia's cone, *Conus juliae* Clench Pinkish with a rather broad white band around the body whorl, this shell is 1½-2 in. (38-51 mm) high, has rounded shoulders, short spire and an overall pattern of fine lines and dots. Rare, this shell is found in moderately deep water from Florida to the West Indies. $20-$60

mouse cone, *Conus mus* Hwass   The shell is gray with reddish-brown spots and usually has a light band around the middle of the body whorl. Surface sculpture is faint spiral cords; height is 1½-2 in. (38-50 mm). Common on sand or reefs in the intertidal zone from southeastern Florida to the West Indies. under $1-$4

Conus peali Green   This ½-¾ in. (13-19 mm) high shell is similar in appearance to *C. jaspideus,* except the color pattern is more subtle. Many malacologists regard this as merely a color variant of *C. jaspideus.* Uncommon, in sand in shallow water from southern Florida to the West Indies. $4

pearled cone, *Conus pennaceus* Born The color of this shell is variable but it is generally orange-brown with white spots and triangular patches. The shell is solid, 2½ in. (64 mm) high and has a moderately raised spire. Fairly common on reefs in Hawaii. $3-$35

68

Conidae

Austin's cone

California cone

Clark's cone

carrot cone

Florida cone

dark Florida cone

Burry's cone

glory-of-the-Atlantic cone

Jasper cone

Julia's cone

mouse cone

Conus peali

pearled cone

cones

Cones (continued)

of the opening. Many species have a heavy periostracum which must be removed to display the colors of the shell. Cones have a harpoon-shaped radula which along with a neurotoxic venom is injected by the proboscis into the victim to aid in its capture. Cone shells live in rocks and coral and are active at night, especially at low tide, feeding on worms, other mollusks, and in the case of some Indo-Pacific species, occasionally on fish. Live cone shells should be handled carefully even though none of the species in our range are dangerous, they can inflict a painful and irritating sting. Only a few Indo-Pacific species are known to inflict fatal wounds on humans.

puzzling cone, *Conus perplexus* Sowerby The gray or pinkish surface of this species is covered with tiny brown dots and has three reddish-brown bands. It is 1 in. (25 mm) high and the pointed spire is heavily marked with brown and white blotches. Common in moderately shallow water from the Gulf of California to South America. under $1-$4

prince cone, *Conus princeps* Linné The yellow-brown shell is marked with irregular brown lines running up and down the body whorl. It is 2½ in. (64 mm) high, has a low spire and thick brown periostracum. Fairly common, found in moderately shallow water from the Gulf of California to Ecuador. $7-$25

Conus pygmaeus, Reeve A white shell usually with dark reddish markings, it has a high spire and is 1-1½ in. (25-38 mm) high. Fairly common, found from Florida to the West Indies. Albino uncommon. $2-$4; albino $9

Conus ranunculus, Hwass A large, colorful cone, it is 2-3 in. (51-76 mm) high, white with reddish-brown markings. Common in Florida and the West Indies. under $1-$2

crown cone, *Conus regius* Gmelin The light colored cone is marked with reddish-brown or purplish mottled patches, sometimes creating a banded appearance. It is 2-3 in. (51-76 mm) high and has knobs on the spire. Common, found on reefs from southern Florida to the West Indies and Brazil. $6-$30

regular cone, *Conus regularis* Sowerby Pale white shell with orange-brown spots, it has a pointed spire and is 2-2½ in. (51-64 mm) high. Fairly common, found in shallow water from the Gulf of California to Panama. $2-$4

Sennott's cone, *Conus sennottorum* Rehder & Abbott This smooth white shell has spiral rows of reddish-brown dots, a prominent spire with a sharp apex, and is 1-1½

in. (25-38 mm) high. Uncommon, found in deep water in the Gulf of Mexico. $60-$200

Sozon's cone, *Conus sozoni* Bartsch The light orange shell has two prominent white bands which have spiral lines made up of brownish dots on the body whorl, and the rest of the shell is marked with reddish-brown splotches. It is 2-4 in. (51-102 mm) high and has a well-developed spire with a sharp apex. Uncommon, found in deep water from South Carolina to Florida and the Gulf of Mexico. $5-$18

alphabet cone, *Conus spurius atlanticus* Clench This is the Florida subspecies of the alphabet cone. It is 2-3 in. (51-76 mm) high, has a flat top with a short spire, and is creamy white with spiral rows of orange and brown spots and blotches. The species has a thin light brown periostracum, feeds on worms, and is fairly common in sand in shallow water from Florida to the West Indies. $5-$50

The Caribbean form, *C. s. spurius,* Gmelin, has darker blotches arranged in more obvious bands. $4-$27; over 3 in. (80 mm) $75

A color variant, *C. s. aureofasciatus,* Rehder & Abbott, occurs, marked with bands of yellow or orange-brown. $1-$2

Stimpson's cone, *Conus stimpsoni* Dall A yellow or white shell, it usually has 2 or 3 yellowish bands around the body whorl, is 1½-2 in. (38-51 mm) high, and has a well formed spire. It is uncommon, found in deep water from southeastern Florida to the Gulf of Mexico. $6

warty cone, *Conus verrucosus,* Hwass This pinkish-gray shell has reddish-brown blotches, regularly placed beads on the revolving ribs, and is ¾-1 in. (19-25 mm) high. Common, in shallow water from southern Florida to the West Indies, Brazil. under $1-$4

puzzling cone

prince cone

Conus pygmaeus

Conus ranunculus

crown cone

regular cone

Sennott's cone

Sozon's cone

alphabet cone

Stimpson's cone

warty cone

Augers (family: *Terebridae*)

Representatives of this family have a long, slender, many-whorled shell with a claw-like operculum which distinguishes them from the similarly shaped members of the *Turritellidae* family, which have a round operculum. These carnivores live in sandy mud or coral sand in shallow water where they feed on sea worms.

gray Atlantic auger, *Terebra cinerea* Born A gray or brown shiny shell, it has numerous small ribs extending vertically halfway down from the sutures on each volution. It is 1-2 in. (25-51 mm) high and has a small aperture. Common, in sandy shallow water from southern Florida to the West Indies and Brazil. $1-$3

common auger, *Terebra dislocata* Say The color of this shell varies from pale gray to orange-brown with darker bands of gray and brown. It is 1-2 in. (25-51 mm) high and has a spiral band just below each suture and numerous axial ribs on each suture. Common in sand in shallow water from Virginia to Florida and the Gulf of Mexico and to the West Indies. under $1-$20

Florida auger, *Terebra floridana* Dall Rather large, 3 in. (76 mm) high, the shell is yellowish white, the whorls have a raised line around the middle and two rows of axial ribs around the top. Rare, found in shallow water from South Carolina to Florida. $10-$20

shiny Atlantic auger, *Terebra hastata* Gmelin Also listed as *Hastula hastata*. This species is not as sharply tapered as other augers. It is 1-1½ in. (25-38 mm) high, glossy tan with a creamy band below the suture. Not common, found in shallow water from southern Florida to the West Indies. $1-$2

Terebra strigata Sowerby Height of this auger is 4 in. (102 mm); it is tan with prominent vertical brown streaks. There is a slight indentation below the well-defined sutures. Not common, found on sand in moderately shallow water from Gulf of California to Panama. $3-$15

flame auger, *Terebra taurinum* Lightfoot Formerly classified as *T. flammaea*, Lamarck. Our largest auger, it reaches a height of 6 in. (152 mm) or more. It is yellowish white with rows of reddish-brown streaks. This uncommon shell is becoming rarer due to overcollecting. It is found in moderately shallow water from southern Florida and the Gulf of Mexico to the West Indies. $5-$20

Turrets (family: *Turridae*)

Also known as turrids and slit shells, members of this family are spindle-shaped, and the outer lip usually has a slit or notch. Generally deep water snails, there are hundreds of species; little is known about them so there is much dispute regarding their classification.

elegant star turret, *Ancistrosyrinx elegans* Dall Up to 2 in. (51 mm) high, this yellowish-white shell has a long open canal, sharply angled volutions with prominent shoulders. There are short spines on the shoulders and the surface has rows of very tiny beads. Rare, found in deep water in southern Florida and the West Indies. $60

Sanibel turret, *Crassispira sanibelensis* Bartsch & Rehder Under 1 in. (25 mm) high, it is pale brown to reddish brown, has a ridge at the suture. Common, found in moderately shallow water in southern Florida and the Gulf of Mexico. under $1

giant white turret, *Polystira albida* Perry A white shell, it has a long open canal, light brown periostracum and a brown claw-like operculum. The shell is 3-4 in. (76-102 mm) high and has a distinct notch on the outer lip. At one time considered rare, it is now frequently found by shrimp fishermen in deep water in southern Florida and the Gulf of Mexico. $2-$5

delicate giant turret, *Polystira tellea* Dall Similar to the giant white turret, but the sculpture of this shell is not as defined. It is grayish or white and 2-3 in. (51-76 mm) high, and has a light brown periostracum. Fairly common in deep water in southeast Florida. $1-$3

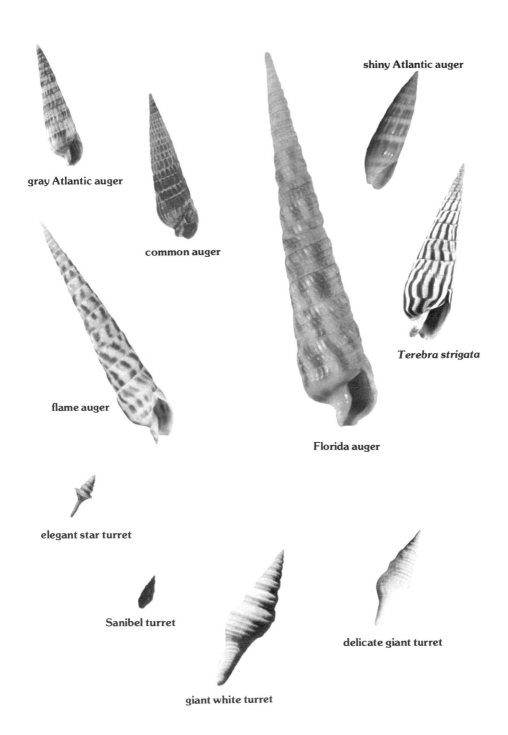

shiny Atlantic auger

gray Atlantic auger

common auger

Terebra strigata

flame auger

Florida auger

elegant star turret

Sanibel turret

delicate giant turret

giant white turret

augers / turrets

Obelisk Shells (family: *Eulimidae*)

These shells have a high spire which is generally slightly bent to one side. The surfaces are polished and the animals are parasites.

obelisk shell, *Niso hendersoni* Bartsch Polished tan or yellowish shell, it is 1 in. (25 mm) high, and suture is marked with darker brown. Uncommon, found in the southeastern part of the United States. $15-$25

Pyramid Shells (family: *Pyramidellidae*)

Pyramid or cone shaped, these shells are usually highly polished. Many of the representatives of this family are tiny. They are found on sandy bottoms and many are parasites.

giant Atlantic pyram, *Pyramidella dolabrata* Lamarck A large representative of this genus, it is 1 in. (25 mm) high, cream-white shell with spiral brown lines on the whorls. The sutures are deeply impressed on this solid shell. Common, found on sand in shallow water from Florida to the West Indies. $2-$3

Lined Bubble Shells (family: *Hydatinidae*)

These snails have thin, rounded, inflated shells with an involute spire. The animal is large, usually extending outside the shell.

brown-lined paper bubble shell, *Hydatina vesicaria* Solander Shell is large, 1-1½ in. (25-38 mm), white to tan with many thin wavy brown lines around the shell. The large colorful animal is rust colored with a blue border. Fairly common in sand in shallow water from southern Florida to the West Indies. $5-$20

True Bubble Shells (family: *Bullidae*)

These oval-shaped shells are thin and lightweight, rolled like a scroll with a wide open aperture. They are carnivores, found in sand and mud bottoms.

bubble shell, *Bulla amygdala* Bruguière A brownish shell with rows of darker brown

spots, it is ¾-1 in. (19-25 mm) high. Common off the west coast of Florida and the West Indies. under $1

California bubble shell, *Bulla gouldiana* Pilsbry Large 1½-2½ in. (38-64 mm) high, this oval grayish-brown shell has dark streaks edged with white. It has a thin brown wrinkled periostracum. Common, found on mud flats at night from the low-tide line to moderately deep water in southern California and the Gulf of Calilfornia. $1-$3

Paper Bubble Shells (family: *Atyidae*)

These small thin shells favor muddy, brackish waters. The animal is large and extends beyond its shell.

paper bubble shell or **elegant glassy bubble,** *Haminoea elegans* Gray This almost transparent shell is thin and fragile, 1/3-3/4 in. (9-19 mm) high, yellowish or cream colored and very glossy. It is common in shallow water from southeast Florida to the West Indies. $1

Sowerby's paper bubble, *Haminoea virescens* Sowerby A small transparent shell about ½ in. (13 mm) high, it is greenish yellow and has a thin outer lip. Uncommon, found among rocks in shallow water from Puget Sound to Mexico. under $1-$2

Marsh Snails (family: *Ellobiidae*)

The shape of these shells varies from conical to round; they lack an operculum. The snails spend a considerable amount of time out of water since their gills have been replaced by a modified lung; however even though they breathe air they stay near salt water.

coffee bean snail, *Melampus coffeus* Linné Brownish gray with 3 white bands on the body whorl, the shell is top shaped and has a gray periostracum. It is ½-¾ in. (13-19 mm) high, has a thin strong shell and low spire. These snails serve as food for wild ducks. Common in intertidal areas in mud near mangroves from southern Florida to the West Indies. under $1

obelisk shell

giant Atlantic pyram

brown-lined paper bubble shell

bubble shell

California bubble shell

paper bubble shell

Sowerby's paper bubble

coffee bean snail

obelisk shell / pyramid shell / lined bubble / true bubbles / paper bubbles / marsh snail

Class: *Amphineura*

Chitons (families: *Chitonidae, Lepidochitonidae*)

The shell of the chiton is made up of 8 overlapping individual plates (valves) which form a shield. The plates are connected by a leathery "girdle" which extends around the plates to form a border. The muscular foot comprises the entire underneath side of the animal. They are nocturnal and are found in rocky areas near shore. Chitons feed on decaying vegetation and some animal matter.

common West Indian chiton, *Chiton tuberculatus* Linné   Color varies from brown to gray and occasionally the shell can be marked with green, black or white. It is 2-3½ in. (51-89 mm) long and the prominent girdle is scaled similar to snakeskin. Common in intertidal zone from Florida to Texas and to the West Indies. $2-$5

lined red chiton, *Tonicella lineata* Wood   The shiny plates are yellowish brown with all or some of the plates decorated on the sides with reddish-brown lines. It is 1 in. (25 mm) long, is found under stones near shore from Alaska to San Diego, California; common on shores of Alaska but uncommon in California. $3-$12

Class: *Scaphopoda*

Tusk Shells (family: *Dentaliidae*)

The animals in this class are covered by a slightly curved tubular shell which is open at both ends. They are found in sand with the smaller end sticking upward while the tough burrowing foot extends from the broad end. The tapered shape of the shell suggests the common name, tusk shell. They are usually white, but can be pale pink or green and are found in sandy bottoms from the intertidal zone to great depths.

ivory tusk shell, *Dentalium eboreum* Conrad   This thin shell is gently curved, 2 in. (51 mm) long, white, occasionally with a pinkish or yellowish cast. Common in shallow water from North Carolina to Florida and to the West Indies.   under $1

Class: *Cephalopoda*

Paper Nautiluses and **Spirula** (families: *Argonautidae, Spirulidae*)

The class *Cephalopoda* includes the most highly evolved mollusks, including the shell-less octopuses and squids, the nautiluses and spirulas. The nautilus is very similar to the octopus. It has eight tentacles, and in the case of the female, two of these arms are modified to produce egg cases and the shell. The female can reach a length of 24 in. (610 mm) and produces a shell about 14 in. (350 mm) long, but the male is shell-less and only about ½ in. (13 mm) long. However, the female is not permanently attached and can discard the shell at any time.

paper nautilus, *Argonauta argo* Linné   The thin shell is white with brown markings around the edge of the early part of the shell. The flat shell reaches a diameter of 8 in. (203 mm). A world-wide pelagic animal, found mostly as empty shells washed on shore from New Jersey to Texas, but primarily off Florida. $10-$225

brown paper nautilus, *Argonauta hians* Lightfoot   The fragile shell is tan or light brown and 2-3 in. (51-76 mm) in diameter. Found world-wide in warm seas, it is occasionally thrown on beaches by storms, primarily off the coasts of Florida and southern California. $1-$7

spirula, *Spirula spirula* Linné   The animal is a squid-like creature with eight arms, two tentacles, and is 1½ in (38 mm) long. This animal produces a white spiral shell, ½-1 in. (13-25 mm) across, which it uses as protection, withdrawing the arms and tentacles into the shell when frightened. The live animal lives at depths of 600-3000 ft. (183-915 m), and the shell floats to the surface when the animal dies and the flesh decays.   under $1-$2

common West Indian chiton

ivory tusk shell

lined red chiton

brown paper nautilus

paper nautilus

spirula

chitons / tusk shell / nautiluses / spirula

Class: *Pelecypoda*

Nut Shells (family: *Nuculidae*)

Shells in this family are thin, have a pearly inside and distinct, sharp interlocking teeth along the hinge. They are usually three-cornered or oval in shape.

Atlantic nut shell, *Nucula proxima* Say
This whitish shell has a thin olive-green periostracum, is almost triangular in shape, and is ¼-⅜ in. (6-10 mm) long. Interior is pearly, with triangular hinge teeth. Common, in mud from Maine to Florida and Texas.   under $1

Nut Shells (family: *Nuculanidae*)

These shells are usually elongated with a rounded front and extended on the other end. They have 2 lines of hinge teeth separated by a large chondrophore.

pointed nut clam, *Nuculana acuta* Conrad
This small shell is ½ in. (13 mm) long, white with a thin brownish or greenish periostracum. The shell has concentric grooves and is pointed on the posterior end. Common, from Massachusetts to Florida and the West Indies.   under $1

Ark Shells (family: *Arcidae*)

Shells in this family are usually heavily ribbed, have a heavy dark periostracum, and lack bright coloration. These strong shells have a hinge that is straight with many small teeth arranged in a line on both valves. Some have a large ventral gape in the shell to accommodate the huge byssus. They can be found attached to undersides of rocks, or in the case of those that lack the byssus, buried in sandy mud.

incongruous ark, *Anadara brasiliana* Lamarck   This shell is 1½-2 in. (38-51 mm) long, about as high, and the left valve is larger and overlaps the other. It is white and has strong ribs marked with crossing lines; periostracum is thin, brown. Common, North Carolina to Florida, Texas, West Indies.   under $1-$2
cut-ribbed ark, *Andara lienosa floridana* Conrad   Formerly classifed as *A. secticostata,* Reeve. This sturdy white shell is 3-5 in. (76-127 mm) long with radiating ribs; periostracum is brown. Common, North Carolina to Florida, Texas, and the West Indies. $2
eared ark, *Anadara notabilis* Röding
The sturdy shell reaches a length of 3½ in. (89 mm), the beaks are well elevated, the anterior end is short and rounded, and the longer posterior end is squarish. It is white with radiating ribs crossed by fine lines; periostracum is brown. Young shells have an obvious dorsal ear. Common, South Carolina to Florida and the West Indies, Brazil. $1-$10
blood ark, *Anadara ovalis* Bruguière
This clam is one of the very few mollusks that has red blood, thus its common name. The shell is 2 in. (51 mm) long, white with the bottom half covered with a greenish-brown thick periostracum. Surface has radiating ribs and the prominent beaks almost touch at the tips. Common, Massachusetts to Florida and Texas, and to the West Indies. $1-$3
mossy ark, *Arca imbricata* Bruguière
Previously classified as *Arca umbonata,* Lamarck. The surface of this 1½-2 in. (38-51 mm) long shell is irregularly criss-crossed by growth lines. It is purplish white inside and out, but is

covered with a dark brown mossy periostracum. Common, North Carolina to Florida and to the West Indies. $1-$2
turkey wing, *Arca zebra* Swainson   This yellowish-white shell is marked with irregular reddish-brown zebra-like stripes. The shell is 2-4 in. (51-102 mm) long, has a moderately large gape, olive-green byssus, and a thick shaggy periostracum which obscures the stripes on live specimens. Common, from North Carolina to Florida, West Indies, Brazil. $1-$2
red-brown ark, *Barbatia cancellaria* Lamarck   This shell is reddish brown with the surface marked with many fine radiating lines; interior is brown. It is 1-2 in. (25-51 mm) long and has a hairy periostracum. Common, from Florida to the West Indies. $1-$2
white-bearded ark, *Barbatia candida* Helbling   Surface of this shell has numerous ribs crossed by growth lines. Shell is 1-2 in. (25-51 mm) long, yellowish white with a shaggy yellowish-brown periostracum. Common, from North Carolina to Florida, Texas, the West Indies. $1-$2

Doc Bale's ark or **stout ark,** *Barbatia tenera* C. B. Adams   About 1½ in. (38 mm) long, this thin white shell has a thin brown periostracum and a sculpture of fine radiating lines. Found in moderately shallow water from southern Florida to the West Indies. $1-$3
ponderous ark, *Noetia ponderosa* Say
A thick shell with strong ribs, it is 2½ in. (64 mm) long, white, with prominent beaks which point backwards. In life it has a heavy, almost black periostracum. Common, from Virginia to Florida and Texas.   under $1-$2

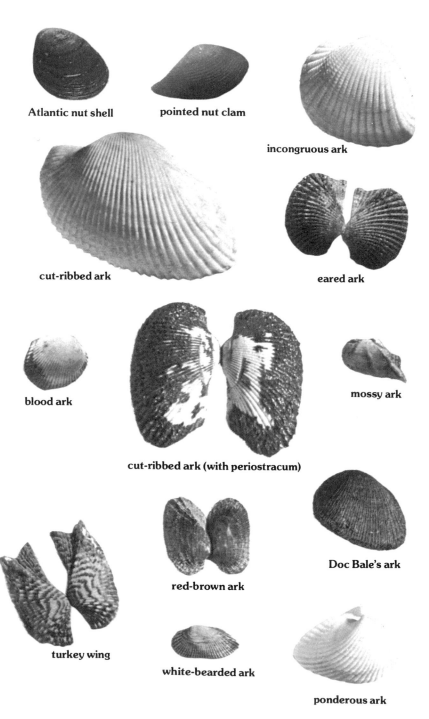

Atlantic nut shell

pointed nut clam

incongruous ark

cut-ribbed ark

eared ark

blood ark

cut-ribbed ark (with periostracum)

mossy ark

turkey wing

red-brown ark

Doc Bale's ark

white-bearded ark

ponderous ark

Bittersweet Clams (family: *Glycymeridae*)

Members of this family are solid, round and well-inflated shells. The hinges have curved rows of teeth, they are colorful, and living shells have a thin velvet-like periostracum which covers most of the shell except near the center of the valves. The distance between the beaks and the direction they turn aid in identification of these clams.

giant American bittersweet, *Glycymeris americana* DeFrance This shell is dull gray or tan, grows up to 5 in. (127 mm) long, is circular and rather compressed, with beaks pointing toward each other. Uncommon, found in moderately shallow to deep water from North Carolina to Florida and Texas. $2-$4

decussate bittersweet, *Glycymeris decussata* Linné The cream colored shell is blotched with brown, has numerous radiating lines and is 1-2 in. (25-51 mm) long. The beaks point toward the rear of the shell. Fairly common, in moderately shallow water from southeast Florida to the West Indies. $1

Glycymeris gigantea Reeve Another large bittersweet, this clam reaches a length of 4 in. (102 mm). It is round, cream colored with reddish-brown mottlings, usually in a zigzag pattern. Uncommon, found in shallow water from the Gulf of California to Acapulco, Mexico $4-$8

comb bittersweet, *Glycymeris pectinata* Gmelin Small, ½-1 in. (12-25 mm) long, this shell is white or gray with bands of brown spots. There are well-rounded radiating ribs. Common, found on sand and gravel in shallow water from North Carolina to Florida and Texas and to the West Indies. $1-$2

Mussels (family: *Mytilidae*)

Members of this family are the true mussels. They are characterized by thin strong pear-shaped shells, a long hinge line and sharp beaks, and shiny interiors. They can be found attached to rocks by the byssus, or attached to underwater objects in communities, forming barriers. Mussels are found in all seas, but do best in cool waters; most are edible.

scorched mussel, *Brachidontes exustus* Linné The elongated gray shell has a yellowish-brown periostracum, is 1 in. (25 mm) long and the surface is ribbed, more prominently near the margins. It is common, often found washed ashore attached to shells and seaweed. It is found in moderately shallow water from Cape Hatteras to Florida and to the West Indies.   under $1

hooked mussel, *Brachidontes recurvus* Rafinesque The valves of this bluish-black shell are triangular and curved. The surface has fine elevated lines which divide as they near the posterior end. This 1-2 in. (25-51 mm) long shell is common, found in shallow water from Cape Cod to Florida, West Indies.   under $1

giant date mussel, *Lithophaga antillarum* d'Orbigny An elongated, cylindrical shell, it is 2-4 in. (51-102 mm) long, has low beaks and no hinge teeth. It is brown, has a thin brown periostracum. Immature species are found hanging from rocks by the byssus; adults bore into limestone and other soft rocks. Fairly common, found in shallow water from southern Florida to the West Indies.   under $1

scissor date mussel, *Lithophaga aristata* Dillwyn This light brown mussel is easily identified by the pointed tips of the valves which cross each other at the posterior end. The elongated shell of this rock borer is 1 in. (25 mm) long. Fairly common, found in soft rocks in moderately shallow water from southern

Florida to the West Indies and Brazil, and from southern California to Peru. $3-$4

tulip mussel, *Modiolus americanus* Leach Previously classified as *Modiolus tulipa,* Lamarck. The thin, strong shell is usually a light brown, but some specimens have fine rose or purple rays; the periostracum is brown. The anterior end is narrow while the posterior end is wide; length is 2-4 in. (51-102 mm). Very common, communities found attached to broken shells and rocks in moderately shallow water from North Carolina to Florida and to the West Indies.   under $1

California mussel, *Mytilus californianus* Conrad Dark brown or bluish-black shell, it is large, attaining a length up to 10 in. (254 mm). It has many irregular radiating ribs, is triangular in shape with the beaks forming a pointy apex. Very common, found on rocks in intertidal area from the Aleutian Islands to California and to Mexico. $1

common blue mussel, *Mytilus edulis* Linné The bluish-black shell has a shiny clear periostracum, reaches a length of 3 in. (76 mm), is triangular shaped with a surface marked by growth lines. This mussel is used as food. Very abundant, it is found in crowded colonies attached to rocks, wharves, by strong byssal threads. An extensive range, it is found in the intertidal zone from Greenland to South Carolina, California, and Europe.   under $1

decussate bittersweet

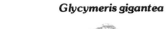
Glycymeris gigantea

giant American bittersweet

comb bittersweet

scorched mussel

hooked mussel

giant date mussel

scissor date mussel

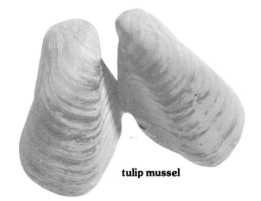

tulip mussel

California mussel

common blue mussel

bittersweet clams / mussels

Pearl Oysters (family: *Pteriidae*)

Members of this family are inequivalve and have an opening under the right valve for the byssus. The tropical species include the valuable pearl oysters which produce gem quality pearls. All species produce mother-of-pearl. Layers of this nacre cover a grain of sand or other small irritant in the mantle, producing a pearl. The larger, more valuable pearls are produced by oysters in Caribbean waters. The pearl oysters are found on rocks, sea fans and other fixed objects.

Atlantic wing oyster, *Pteria colymbus* Röding   The shell is purplish brown with brown radiating lines and has a pearly interior. It is fairly solid, has a straight hinge line and is 1½-3 in. (38-76 mm) long. The matted spiny periostracum is usually rubbed off of more mature specimens. Left valve is inflated, right flattened. Common, found in shallow water attached to sea fans and sea whips from North Carolina to the West Indies, Brazil. $1

western wing oyster, *Pteria sterna* Gould Similar to the Atlantic wing oyster, this shell is purplish brown with lighter brown rays and has a long posterior wing, differentiating it from the Atlantic species. The western wing oyster was once a commercial source for mother-of-pearl. The shell is 3-4 in. (76-102 mm) long and has a wrinkled periostracum. Fairly common, found among weeds in muddy shallow water from California to Panama. $1-$4

Atlantic pearl oyster, *Pinctada radiata* Leach   The color of this shell varies, but it is usually some shade of brown or green. The shell is flat, thin and brittle, 2-3 in. (51-76 mm) long, has a tan periostracum, occasionally with long fine spines if the specimen is found in quiet waters. Common, in shallow water attached to rocks and sea fans from southern Florida to the West Indies, Brazil. $1-$3

Flat Oysters and Tree Oysters (family: *Isognomonidae*)

Characterized by vertical parallel grooves on the external hinge area, these oysters are compressed or flattened with one valve flatter than the other, thin-shelled, and smooth, although in some cases they have concentric plate-like growth lines. They can be almost circular, or oval, or elongated into a hammer-like shape. The flat oysters attach themselves to undersides of rocks, crevices, mangrove roots, by means of a byssus.

flat tree oyster, *Isognomon alatus* Gmelin Valves of this almost circular shell are extremely flat, marked with growth lines that may be smooth or rough. The color varies from brown, black or purplish and it is 2-3 in. (51-76 mm) long. Common, found in large clumps on mangrove roots, pilings, or submerged brush in shallow water from southern Florida to the West Indies, Brazil. $1

Lister's tree oyster, *Isognomon radiatus* Anton   Previously classified as *I. listeri*. An elongated shell, irregular in shape, it reaches a length of 3 in. (76 mm), has flat wrinkled valves, and is greenish brown. Common, under rocks and in crevices from the low-tide line to moderately shallow water from southeastern Florida to the West Indies, and to Brazil. under $1

Pen Shells (family: *Pinnidae*)

These shells are large, wedge shaped with thin shells that gape at the posterior end. They are found partially buried in sand, attached by a strong byssus. Some species attain a length of more than 2½ feet (762 mm).

stiff pen shell, *Atrina rigida* Solander A large delicate shell, it can attain a length of 12 in. (305 mm). The triangular shell is dark brown and the valves have many rows of tube-like spines on slightly elevated ribs, and has a strong silky byssus. Fairly common, it is found in shallow muddy water from North Carolina to Florida and the West Indies. $2

Atlantic wing oyster

western wing oyster (underside)

Atlantic pearl oyster

flat tree oyster

Lister's tree oyster

stiff pen shell

pearl oysters / tree oysters / flat oysters / pen shell

Scallops (family: *Pectinidae*)

All scallops were previously classified in one genus, *Pecten*. However, because of the great diversity of the members, many genera have been derived for classification of this family. Scallops usually are inequivalve, having a strongly convex lower valve and a flat or concave upper valve. The surface usually bears ribs and the margins of the valves are

(continued on page 86)

calico scallop, *Aequipecten gibbus* Linné These little scallops are extremely variable in color—the upper valve can be a mixture of white, rose, purple, brown, yellow-orange, and the bottom valve is usually whitish with flecks of color. Length is 1-2 in. (25-51 mm), wings are equal, and the valves have many radiating ribs crossed by growth lines. This scallop is harvested commercially for food. Common, in shallow water from North Carolina to Florida and the Gulf of Mexico and to the West Indies. $1-$7

Tryon's scallop, *Aequipecten glyptus* Verrill This pinkish-brown shell has a darker color on the radial flutings; length is 1-2½ in. (38-51 mm). Valves are concave; right valve and interior are white. Uncommon, found from south of Cape Cod to Florida and the Gulf of Mexico. $2-$12

Atlantic bay scallop, *Aequipecten irradians* Lamarck Pictured is *A. i. irradians*, an east coast subspecies. Length of the shell is 2-3 in. (51-76 mm), wings are equal, and valves are convex. The grayish-brown subspecies has rounded radiating ribs and mottlings on both similarly colored valves. This species is the common commercial scallop of the east coast. Common, found in eelgrass from Nova Scotia to Florida. under $1-$3

The Gulf subspecies, *A. i. amplicatus*, Dall, is found in the Gulf of Mexico. It is mottled gray to black with a white lower valve. The shell is very inflated. Common in Texas. $1-$2

Another subspecies, *A. i. concentricus*, Say, is not pictured. It is more brightly colored, usually orange-brown to bluish-gray upper valve, light colored lower valve. Common from New Jersey to Florida and along the Gulf coast to Louisiana. under $1-$3

wavy-lined scallop, *Aequipecten lineolaris* Lamarck Tan with wavy concentric lines and prominent dark spots, it is 1-2 in. (25-51 mm) long. Uncommon, its range is from the Florida Keys to the West Indies. $2-$6

rough scallop, *Aequipecten muscosus* Wood The many ribs on the valves are very heavily scaled, shell is sturdy, wings are unequal, and length is 1-2 in. (25-51 mm). Color is variable from tan to orange to reddish brown, and, rarely, bright lemon yellow. Moderately common in fairly shallow water from North Carolina to Florida and the West Indies. $1-$4; orange $15; yellow $8

spathate scallop, *Aequipecten phrygium* Dall A flat, fan-shaped shell 1 in. (25 mm) long. Valves are gray with irregular pinkish bands and have prominent ribs. Rare, in deep water from Cape Cod to eastern Florida and to the West Indies. $30-$75

Pacific pink scallop, *Chlamys hastata hericius* Gould The shell is almost round, with the front wings twice as large as the hind wings, and is 2-3¼ in. (51-83 mm) high. The valves can be white, yellow, orange or purple, usually with paler colors on the rays or marked by purple rings. Fairly common on rocks, sand or mud, or in sponges from the low-tide line to deep water from southern Alaska to California. $1-$6; orange $35

little knobby scallop, *Chlamys imbricatus* Gmelin Length is 1-1¾ in. (25-44 mm), the valves of this shell are usually flat, white, sometimes with patches of pink, and the margins and hinge area are purplish. Wings are unequal and the ribs have regularly spaced hollow knobs. Rare, found in moderately shallow water from southern Florida to the West Indies. $6-$15

Mildred's scallop, *Chlamys mildredae* Bayer A tan to brown shell with strong radiating ribs and unequal wings, this shell is about 1 in. (25 mm) long. Rare, found in southeast Florida to the Gulf of Mexico and off Bermuda. $25-$125

ornate scallop, *Chlamys ornatus* Lamarck Small, 1-1¼ in. (25-32 mm) long, wings are extremely unequal—one barely discernible. Strongly ribbed, the shell is brown or tan, or white with brown or red spots. Uncommon, found in shallow water from southern Florida to the West Indies. $3-$12

sentis scallop, *Chlamys sentis* Reeve Valves of this species are quite flat with many fine ribs, and the front wings are 4-5 times larger than the hind wings. The shell is 1-1½ in. (25-38 mm) long and the color varies from orange to purplish, yellowish. Common, found attached to undersides of rocks from North Carolina to the Florida Keys and West Indies. $1-$3

Benedict's scallop, *Chlamys benedicti*, Verrill & Busch, (unpictured) is similar but is smaller and has larger hind wings. It is found from southern Florida to Texas and is not as common. $2-$10

calico scallop

Tryon's scallop

wavy-lined scallop

Atlantic bay scallop
(east coast subspecies)

Atlantic bay scallop
(Gulf subspecies)

rough scallop

spathate scallop

Pacific pink scallop

Mildred's scallop

little knobby scallop

ornate scallop

sentis scallop

Scallops (continued)

scalloped. In live specimens the outer edge of the mantle has a row of tiny eyes, each with a cornea, lens and optic nerve. Juveniles are sedentary, usually fixed by a byssus. Most adult species however, are capable of swimming by rapidly opening and closing the valves, which propels the scallop through the water—backwards—with the hinge end trailing. The large mussel which controls this movement of the valves is the part we eat when we have "scallops". Several species are commercially valuable as food.

giant rock scallop, *Hinnites multirugosus* Gale   Also classified as *H. giganteus,* Gray. The shell is reddish brown to light gray with the colors fading as the shell grows. This scallop begins life as a free-swimming bivalve, but becomes sessile, attaching itself by the lower valve to rocks. The shell is thick with many small scaly ribs, oyster-like in appearance, and is 3-10 in. (76-254 mm) long. Common, found on rocks from the low-tide line to moderately shallow water from the Aleutian Islands to Baja California. $3-$7

Antillean scallop, *Lyropecten antillarum* Récluz   This small shell is usually under 1 in. (25 mm) long, has thin rather flat valves with quite widely spaced ribs. Color may be light yellow, pale orange or tan, occasionally with white mottlings. Fairly common in shallow water from southern Florida to the West Indies. Colored shells are rare. $2-$6; colors $10

lion's paw, *Lyropecten nodosus* Linné This heavy shell is reddish brown to orange, 4-6 in. (102-152 mm) long, has strong ribs with prominent raised knobs. A prized collector's item; while it is fairly common, only single shells are usually found washed up on shore. Found in moderately deep water from North Carolina to Florida and the Gulf of Mexico and to the West Indies, Brazil. $4-$175

giant Pacific scallop or **weathervane scallop,** *Pecten caurinus* Gould   The valves are flat, thick and solid, have broad sturdy ribs; wings are equal. It reaches a length of 6-8 in. (152-203 mm); upper valve is purplish red and lower valve is pink or white. This species is fished commercially. Fairly common in moderately deep water from Alaska to Humboldt Bay, California. $8-$10

Pecten laurenti Gmelin   The upper valve is slightly convex, tan or light reddish brown with white mottlings; the lower valve is more convex and white. Wings are about equal and the shell

is 2½ in. (64 mm) long. Uncommon, found in the Gulf of Mexico and Caribbean. $2-$8

paper scallop, *Pecten papyraceus* Gabb Upper valve is flat, glossy, smooth and reddish brown; lower valve is white with a rim of yellow on the inside, occasionally on the outside of the valve. It is 2 in. (51 mm) long and does not have ribs. Fairly common, found in moderately deep water from the Gulf of Mexico to the West Indies. $5-$7

Ravenel's scallop, *Pecten raveneli* Dall The shell is pink to purple, only occasionally orange. Upper valve is flat with dark irregular markings; lower valve is convex and has many widely separated grooved ribs. It is 2 in. (51 mm) long and has unequal wings. Uncommon, found in moderately shallow water from North Carolina to the West Indies. $1-$4; purple/ orange $5-$12; albino $10

tereinus scallop, *Pecten tereinus* Dall Small, about 1 in. (25 mm) long, this scallop is grayish white or buff with irregular tan markings. Uncommon, found from southern Florida to the Gulf of Mexico. $5-$17

zigzag scallop, *Pecten ziczac* Linné Length of this shell is 2-4 in. (51-102 mm), the upper valve is flat, has many compressed ribs and is blotched and marked with zigzag black lines; the lower convex valve has low ribs and is mottled reddish brown. Common, in moderately shallow water from North Carolina to Florida and the West Indies; Bermuda. $1-$25

Atlantic deep-sea scallop, *Placopecten magellanicus* Gmelin   Large, 5-8 in. (127-203 mm) long, the valves are flat and roughened with many narrow radiating ribs. Wings are equal; upper valve reddish or pinkish brown; lower valve is a warm white. Common, this species is fished commercially. Found in moderately deep water from Labrador to North Carolina. $4-$13; albino $15-$25

giant Pacific scallop

giant rock scallop

Antillean scallop

Pecten laurenti

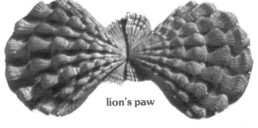
lion's paw

tereinus scallop

paper scallop

Ravenel's scallop

zigzag scallop

Atlantic deep-sea scallop

File Shells (family: *Limidae*)

These oval shells have long colorful sticky tentacles protruding from the shell in the live specimens. Usually they have only one wing and gape open on one side. They can swim in the manner of the scallops, but forwards, hinge first. However they are usually sedentary.

spiny file shell or **spiny lima**, *Lima lima* Linné A white shell with many spined ribs, it is 1-1½ in. (25-38 mm) long; byssal gape is small; anterior wing larger. Common, from southeast Florida to the West Indies. $1-$2

delicate file shell, *Lima scabra tenera* Sowerby This thick oval shell is 1-3 in. (25-76 mm) long and the surface has numerous small ribs giving the shell a satin-like luster. It is white, with a thin yellow-tan periostracum. Common from Florida to West Indies. $1

The rough lima, *Lima scabra scabra,* Born (not pictured), has many ribs which are covered with small spines. $2-$4

Spiny Oysters (family: *Spondylidae*)

Most members of this family live attached by their right valves to rocks in shallow to moderately deep water. Like the scallops, they have eyes along the edge of the mantle. The shells develop long spines, usually in quiet waters.

Atlantic spiny oyster or **thorny oyster,** *Spondylus americanus* Hermann Color is variable from white to brown, and occasionally yellow or red. The heavy shell is 3-5 in. (76-127 mm) and is covered with radiating ribs and spines. Although these shell are common, the specimens found on beaches or in coral are usually badly worn. Found on coral from Florida to the West Indies. $9-$50

Spondylus gussoni Da Costa A brown spiny shell, 2-4 in. (51-102 mm) long, it is found in the Gulf of Mexico. $7-$13

Cat's Paws (family: *Plicatulidae*)

These small, thick shells are identified by the broad radiating ribs or folds. They are found on rocks and coral where they are attached by either valve.

cat's paw or **kitten's paw,** *Plicatula gibbosa* Lamarck Usually 1 in. (25 mm) long or smaller, this white shell has pencil-like gray or reddish lines on the radiating folds. But most are white because the sun bleaches them. Very common from North Carolina to Florida and to the West Indies. $1

Oysters (family: *Ostreidae*)

These are extremely irregularly shaped shells with unequal valves. They are usually fixed by the lower valve to some solid object. They produce nonvaluable pearls.

Ostrea cristata, Born A Caribbean species of oyster, is is 1-2 in. (25-51 mm) long. under $1

crested oyster, *Ostrea equestris* Say The oval shaped shell is 2 in. (51 mm) long, whitish, covered with a brown or grayish-purple periostracum. Common, Virginia to Florida and Texas, West Indies. $1

coon oyster, *Ostrea frons* Linné Shape of this oyster is variable: it is long when attached to stems, rounded when on rocks. It is reddish to deep brown, 1½-2 in. (38-51 mm) long. Common from North Carolina to Florida and to the West Indies. $1-$2

native Pacific oyster, *Ostrea lurida* Carpenter Shape of the shell varies, but it is usually small, 2 in. (51 mm) long, with a rough surface and crude growth lines. The brownish-gray oyster is excellent eating. Common, Alaska to Baja California. $1

sponge oyster, *Ostrea permollis* Sowerby This oyster lives in the sponge, *Stellata sp.* It is 1-3 in. (25-76 mm) long, whitish or tan with irregular wavy ridges and a thick soft periostracum. Common from North Carolina to Florida and the West Indies. $2-$3

giant Pacific oyster, *Crassostrea gigas* Thurnberg Large, gray or tan shell up to 12 in. (305 mm) long, it is variable in shape, usually elongated with coarse surface sculpture. Native to Japan, it was introduced in Hawaii, and from British Columbia to California. $1-$4

eastern oyster, *Crassostrea virginica* Gmelin This is the most important commercial oyster. It is 3-6 in. (76-152 mm) long, dark gray, and the shell is rough and heavy. Shape varies depending on its position as it grows, often in dense colonies. Common from New Brunswick to Florida, Gulf of Mexico; introduced on Pacific coast of U.S. $1-$3

Jingle Shells (family: *Anomiidae*)

These thin, translucent clams have a stalk-like byssus which fixes the shell through a hole in the lower valve. When the animal dies, the cup-like upper valve is washed ashore.

jingle shell, *Anomia simplex* d'Orbigny Color varies from dull yellow to coppery red or even gray or black. The shell is 1-2 in. (25-51 mm) long. Common from Nova Scotia to Florida and to the West Indies. $1-$3

spiny file shell

delicate file shell

Atlantic spiny oyster

Spondylus gussoni

cat's paw

Ostrea cristata

crested oyster

coon oyster
(on stem with barnacle)

native Pacific oyster

sponge oyster

giant Pacific oyster

eastern oyster

jingle shell

Arctic Clams (family: Arcticidae)

This family has many fossil genera but only one surviving species. The shells are large, thick, circular and have a thick periostracum. They live buried in sand with only the end of the short siphon exposed.

black clam or **ocean quahog,** *Arctica island-ica* Linné   Large, up to 4 in. (102 mm) long, the whitish shell has a dark wrinkled periostracum. Common, large colonies are dredged in moderately deep water from the Arctic Ocean to North Carolina. $7-$8

Marsh Clams (family: Corbiculiidae)

These clams favor brackish water and are eaten by waterfowl. The thick inflated shells can be round or triangular.

Carolina marsh clam, *Polymesoda caroliniana* Bosc   This shell is olive to greenish brown and has a thin brown periostracum. Round, 1-2 in. (25-51 mm) long; common, in mud from Virginia to Florida, Texas. under $1

Astartes (family: Astartidae)

These bivalves have an external ligament, distinct lunule, and are sculp-tured with concentric grooves; most have a tough brown periostracum.

boreal astarte, *Astarte borealis* Schumacher   This white shell is solid, oval, 1-2½ in. (25-64 mm) long, and the periostracum is usually frayed at the margins. Common, from the Arctic to Massachusetts and to Alaska.   under $1

Crassatellas (family: Crassatellidae)

These clams are solid with equal valves and strong hinges.

Gibb's clam, *Eucrassatella speciosa* Adams   A brown shell with a thin brown periostracum, it has many dense packed ridges. It is 2 in. (51 mm) long with a round anterior, and a ridge on the hind end. Common from North Carolina to Florida and to the West Indies. $1-$2

Carditas (family: Carditidae)

These are usually solid, equivalve, and strongly ribbed shells with a strong triangular tooth under the right umbo.

broad-ribbed cardita, *Cardita floridana* Conrad   White or grayish shell has raised beaded radial ribs with reddish-brown spots; periostracum is gray. It is 1-1½ in. (25-38 mm). Common, Florida to Texas, Mexico. under $1

Lucines and Buttercups (family: Lucinidae)

These shell are usually round, rather thick, and are white or yellowish. They live in sand or mud where the animal constructs a mucus-lined tube to draw water and food, and expels wastes through a siphon.

buttercup lucine, *Anodontia alba* Link   White shell has fine concentric growth lines, orange bands, and interior has an orange cast. It is 1½-2 in. (38-51 mm) long, common from North Carolina to Florida, Gulf states, and the West Indies. $3

chalky buttercup, *Anodontia philippiana* Reeve   Was listed as *A. schrammi* or *Loripinus schrammi,* Crosse. White with fine concentric lines, it is 2-4 in. (51-102) mm long; interior is colorless. Common, from North Carolina to the West Indies.   under $1

Californian lucine, *Codakia californica* Conrad   Also listed as *Epilucina californica.* Dull white with many fine concentric ridges, it is 1-2½ in. (25-64 mm) long. Common, southern California to Baja California. $7-$8

tiger lucine, *Codakia orbicularis* Linné   White shell is marked with many fine radiating ribs crossed by raised growth lines. It is 2½-3½ in. (64-89 mm) long, and may have a pink border on the inside. Common from Florida to the West Indies. $2

cross-hatched lucine, *Divaricella quadrisulcata* d'Orbigny   White, 1 in. (25 mm) long, with parallel grooves running diagonally across the surface. Common, in moderately shallow water from Massachusetts to Florida and to the West Indies.   under $1

northeast lucine, *Lucina filosus* Stimpson   Was listed as *Phacoides filosus.* White, 1-3 in. (25-76 mm) long, the compressed valves have widely spaced concentric ridges. Prefers cold water. Common from Newfoundland to Florida.   under $1

Florida lucine, *Lucina floridana* Conrad   White with a thin yellow periostracum, it is 1½ in. (38 mm) long, and the thick valves have fine concentric lines. Common in shallow water in the Gulf of Mexico.   under $1

thick lucine, *Lucina pectinatus.* Gmelin   Was listed as *Phacoides pectinatus.* A heavy yellowish-white shell, 1½-2 in. (38-51 mm) long, has fine concentric ridges and an obvious fold on the hind end. Common from North Carolina to Florida, the West Indies.   under $1

Pennsylvania lucine, *Lucina pensylvanica* Linné   White with pale yellow or tan periostracum, it has widely spaced concentric ridges, a deep fold from the beak to the posterior margin, and is 1-2 in. (25-51 mm). Common, North Carolina to Florida, West Indies. $1-$2

black clam

Carolina marsh clam

boreal astarte

Gibb's clam

broad-ribbed
cardita

buttercup lucine

chalky buttercup

Californian lucine

tiger lucine

cross-hatched lucine

northeast lucine

Florida lucine

thick lucine

Pennsylvania lucine

Jewel Boxes (family: *Chamidae*)

Jewel boxes are thick, heavy shells that have unequal valves and sometimes produce long spine-like projections similar to the spiny oysters. They live attached to rocks, corals, shells, or other solid objects, by means of the fixed valve which is the larger and more convex.

leafy jewel box, *Chama macerophylla* Gmelin   The color of ths shell varies from yellow and pink to rose. It is 1-3 in. (25-76 mm) long, and the surface has large, scale-like projections with tiny radial lines. Common, found in shallow to moderately shallow water from North Carolina to the West Indies. $1-$8

clear jewel box, *Chama pellucida* Broderip Also classified as *Chama arcana*. Usually white or cream, it can be tinged with pink or orange, with the overall appearance of the shell being translucent. It is 1½-3½ in. (38-89 mm) long, and has numerous leafy concentric ridges with irregular leafy projections. Common, found attached to rocks and pilings in shallow to moderately deep water from Oregon to Peru. $2-$13

smooth-edged jewel box, *Chama sinuosa* Broderip   This shell is always white, usually with a greenish interior. It is 2-2½ (51-64 mm) long, very similar to the leafy jewel box, except the margin inside of the valves is smooth. Uncommon, found on coral reefs in moderately deep water from southern Florida to the West Indies. $2-$4

Caribbean spiny jewel box, *Echinochama arcinella* Linné   Also listed as *Arcinella arcinella*. This yellowish-white shell is about 1 in. (25 mm) long, and usually has a pinkish tinge on the inside of the valves. Common, found in shallow water from the West Indies to South America. $2

Florida spiny jewel box, *Echinochama cornuta* Conrad   Also listed as *Arcinella cornuta*. About 1½ in. (38 mm) long, this shell is very similar to the Caribbean spiny jewel box, but it is larger. It is white, with the interior often having tinges of red. Common in shallow water from North Carolina to Florida and Texas. $2

Cockles (family: *Cardiidae*)

When viewed from the end, these bivalves are heart shaped. The valves are equal with serrated or scalloped margins and often gape at one end. They are edible and are popular as food in Europe.

Nuttall's cockle, *Clinocardium nuttalli* Conrad   Shell is whitish or yellowish with a light brown or yellowish-brown periostracum. A large, almost circular shell, 2-5½ in. (51-140 mm) long, the beaks are high and the valves are sculptured with strong ribs. Common, found in moderately shallow water from the Bering Sea to San Diego, California. $9-$10

giant Atlantic cockle, *Dinocardium robustum* Lightfoot   This rather heavy, inflated shell is 3-5 in. (76-127 mm) long. The valves have regularly spaced strong ribs and rounded beaks. Color is yellowish or tan with irregular spots; interior is rose. Common, found in moderately shallow water or washed up on shore from Virginia to Florida and Texas. $3

common heart cockle, *Dinocardium robustum vanhyningi* Clench and Smith   This subspecies of the giant Atlantic cockle is generally larger, more colorful and more triangular in shape than *D. robustum*. It is very common, found in moderately shallow water off the west coast of Florida.   under $1

giant Pacific egg cockle, *Laevicardium elatum* Sowerby   One of the largest cockles, this shell reaches a length of 6 in. (152 mm). The thin valves are inflated and have weak radiating ribs, giving the yellow shell a rather smooth surface. Fairly common, in moderately shallow water from southern California to Panama. $4-$15

clear jewel box

leafy jewel box

smooth-edged jewel box

Caribbean spiny jewel box

Florida spiny jewel box

Nuttall's cockle

giant Atlantic cockle

common heart cockle

giant Pacific egg cockle

Cockles (continued)

egg cockle, *Laevicardium laevigatum* Linné The thin shell is inflated, 1-2 in. (25-51 mm) long, white with concentric bands of yellow-orange. Surface is smooth with slight traces of ribs; periostracum is thin and brownish. Occasional colorful specimens may be found, but most are white. Common, found in moderately shallow water from North Carolina to both coasts of Florida and to the West Indies. under $1-$2

Morton's egg cockle, *Laevicardium mortoni* Conrad   This shell is small, ¾ in. (19 mm) long, yellowish white with occasional streaks of orange. The shell is inflated, thin, and has a slightly pebbled surface. Common, found in sandy mud from the low-tide line to moderately shallow water from Cape Cod to both Florida coasts and to the West Indies. under $1

Ravenel's egg cockle, *Laevicardium pictum* Ravenel   A white smooth shell, some specimens are marked with brown zigzag streaks. The well inflated shell is small, ¾ in. (19 mm) long. Fairly common, found in moderately shallow water from South Carolina to Florida and the West Indies. under $1-$2

little egg cockle, *Laevicardium substriatum* Conrad   Another small cockle, about 1 in. (25 mm) long, the valves are thin, inflated and quite smooth; color is yellowish brown with a yellow interior spotted with purple. Common, found in moderately shallow water from Catalina Island, California to Baja California. under $1

spiny paper cockle, *Papyridea soleniformis* Bruguière   The interior and exterior of this shell is white or pink, mottled with rosy brown; rare specimens are orange. It is 1½ in. (38 mm) long, thin and flat with numerous fine radiating ribs. Fairly common, found in shallow water from North Carolina to Florida and to the West Indies. $1-$2

prickly cockle, *Trachycardium egmontianum* Shuttleworth   The surface has deep radiating ribs which end in sharp scales. The shell is thin, oval, well inflated, 2-2½ in. (51-64 mm) long, yellowish; rarely, albino. Common, found in sand in shallow water from North Carolina to Florida. under $1-$5

West Indies prickly cockle, *Trachycardium isocardia* Linné   Reaches a length of 3 in. (76 mm), this shell is yellow with irregular brown blotches and has strong radiating ribs with sharp scales. Common, found in shallow water in the West Indies. $1

magnum cockle, *Trachycardium magnum* Linné   White or cream colored shell, it is marked with yellowish-brown patches, sculptured with deep radiating ribs, and is 2-3½ in. (51-89 mm) long. Uncommon, found from the lower Florida Keys to the West Indies. $2-$6

yellow cockle or **lemon cockle,** *Trachycardium muricatum* Linné   The shell is almost round, yellowish white, occasionally with light speckles. It is strongly inflated, 2 in. (51 mm) long, and has spiny radiating ribs; the periostracum is brown. Very common, found in shallow water from North Carolina to Florida and Texas, and to the West Indies. $1-$5

Atlantic strawberry cockle, *Trigoniocardia media* Linné   Also listed as *Americardia media.* A cream colored shell, the surface is checkered with brown to reddish-brown and has strong rounded radiating ribs. Length is 1-2 in. (25-51 mm). Common, found in shallow to moderately deep water from North Carolina to Florida and to the West Indies. $2-$5

The western strawberry cockle, *Trigonicardia biangulata* or *Americardia biangulata,* Broderip & Sowerby (not pictured), is similar, but found off California. under $1-$3

egg cockle

little egg cockle

Ravenel's egg cockle

Morton's egg cockle

spiny paper cockle

prickly cockle

West Indies prickly cockle

magnum cockle

yellow cockle

Atlantic strawberry cockle

Hard-shelled Clams (family: *Veneridae*)

The hundreds of species in this very large family have certain obvious characteristics: the shells are porcelain-like, equivalve, egg- or heart-shaped; beaks point toward the anterior; ligament is external and hinge is strong; each valve has three cardinal teeth. Many have beautiful sculpture and are brightly colored. They burrow and are usually found just below the surface of the sand. These clams are an important commercial food fishery.

pointed venus, *Anomalocardia cuneimeris* Conrad   Wedge shaped, thin, ¾ in. (19 mm) long, the color varies from grayish to greenish or brownish. It has many concentric ribs and is pointed at one end. Common, from southern Florida to Texas.   under $1

rigid venus, *Antigona rigida* Dillwyn Also *Ventricolaria rigida.* Yellowish-gray mottled with brown, 1½-2½ in. (38-63 mm) long, it has alternating concentric ribs and smaller lines. Common, from southern Florida to the West Indies. $1

queen venus, *Antigona rugatina,* Heilprin Also *Ventricolaria rugatina.* Shell is yellowish-white with brown mottlings, 1-1½ in. (25-38 mm) long, with concentric ribs separated by two fine lines. Rare, North Carolina to Florida and the West Indies. $5-$8

empress venus, *Antigona strigillina* Dall Cream colored, 1½ in. (38 mm) long, it has raised concentric ribs crossed by many fine radiating ribs. Uncommon, South Carolina to Florida and the West Indies. $4

glory-of-the-sea venus, *Callista eucymata* Dall   May be shiny white to shiny pale brown with reddish-brown marks, it is 1-1½ in. (25-38 mm) long, with flat concentric ribs. Rare, North Carolina to Florida, Texas, West Indies. $4

common California venus, *Chione californiensis* Broderip   Gray with concentric ridges and radial ribs, it is 1½-3 in. (38-76 mm). Common, California to Panama. $2-$3

cross-barred venus, *Chione cancellata* Linné   Whitish-gray shell, 1-1½ in. (25-38 mm), it has concentric and radial ribs. Common, North Carolina to Florida, West Indies. $1-$2

beaded venus, *Chione granulata* Gmelin Gray with dark mottlings, close scaly radiating ribs, it is 1 in. (25 mm) long. Common from southern Florida to the West Indies. $1-$2

lady-in-waiting venus, *Chione intapurpurea* Conrad   A whitish thick shell, concentric ribs are wrinkled on hind end, it is 1-1½ in. (25-38 mm). Common, North Carolina to Florida, Gulf states, and the West Indies. $1-$2

imperial venus, *Chione latilirata* Conrad Polished grayish-white shell with brown and purple marks, it has large, broadly rounded concentric ribs and is 1-2 in. (25-51 mm) long. Common, North Carolina to Florida, Texas, and the West Indies. $1-$3; albino $3-$4

Chione mazycki Dall   Grayish-white shell, 1-1½ in. (25-38 mm), brown spots, concentric ribs. North Carolina to Florida. $2-$3

king venus, *Chione paphia* Linné   Shiny, gray marked with purple and brown, 1½ in. (38 mm) long, the shell has narrower concentric ribs than the imperial venus. Fairly common, southeast Florida to the West Indies. $2-$4

elegant dosinia, *Dosinia elegans* Conrad White shell with many concentric ridges, 2-3 in. (51-76 mm). Common, Gulf states. $1 or less

calico clam, *Macrocallista maculata* Linné Tan, checkered with brown 2-3 in. (51-76 mm) long. Fairly common, North Carolina to Florida and the West Indies. $1-$4

sunray venus, *Macrocallista nimbosa* Lightfoot   Pinkish gray with darker radiating markings, it reaches 6 in. (152 mm). Common, North Carolina to Florida, Texas. $2-$3

quahog or **cherrystone clam,** *Mercenaria mercenaria* Linné   A valuable commerical clam, it attains 5-6 in. (127-152 mm); the thick shell is dull gray, often with a purple border. Very common, Gulf of St. Lawrence to Florida, introduced in California. $1-$2

Two subspecies include *M. m. notata,* Say, brightly colored with zigzag marks; and the fatter Texas quahog, *M. m. texana,* Dall. $1-$4

princess venus, *Periglypta listeri* Gray Was listed as *Antigona listeri.* Thick, grayish white, 2-4 in. (51-102 mm), radial ribs, concentric ridges. Florida to West Indies. $2-$3

royal comb venus, *Pitar dione* Linné   Pale violet or white, it has a long ridge at the posterior, 1½ in. (38 mm) long. Common from Texas, Florida to the West Indies. $4-$5

Pitar lupanaria Less   Similar to *P. dione,* but 2 in. (51 mm) and it has concentric ribs. Uncommon, Gulf of California to Peru. $3-$8

Pacific littleneck, *Protothaca staminea* Conrad   Cream to brown, may have brownish mottlings, 2 in. (51 mm), and it has many concentric and radial ribs. Common, Alaska to Baja California. $1

Washington clam, *Saxidomus nuttalli* Conrad   Grayish white with irregular brown lines, up to 5 in. (127 mm), and has fine, sharp concentric ribs. Common, California. $1

trigonal tivela, *Tivela mactroides* Born Triangular, yellowish brown with darker radiating rays, it is 1 in. (25 mm) long. Common, in the West Indies. $1-$2

Veneridae

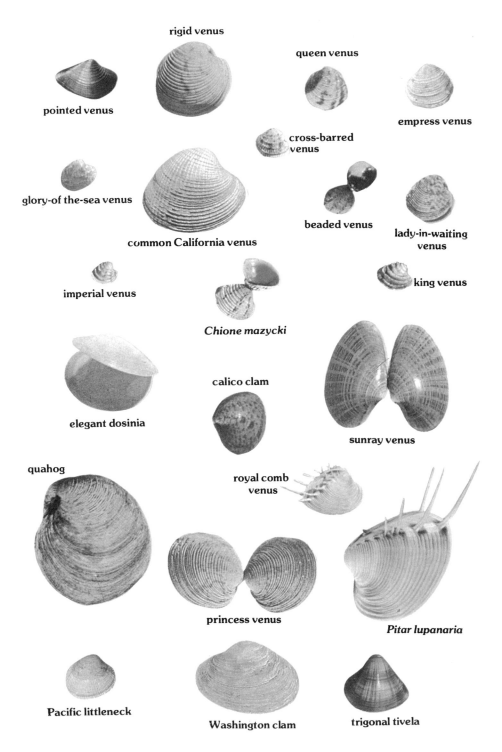

rigid venus

pointed venus

queen venus

empress venus

cross-barred venus

glory-of the-sea venus

common California venus

beaded venus

lady-in-waiting venus

imperial venus

Chione mazycki

king venus

elegant dosinia

calico clam

sunray venus

quahog

royal comb venus

princess venus

Pitar lupanaria

Pacific littleneck

Washington clam

trigonal tivela

Rock Dwellers (family: *Petricolidae*)

The mollusks in this family burrow in clay, shale, coral or limestone, creating a cavity which is enlarged as the clam grows to full adult size. Large communities of these shells can cause erosion of shore lines. The shells are elongated, have a weak hinge, and gape behind.

false angel wing, *Petricola pholadiformis* Lamarck   The thin, long shell has many strong radiating ribs, is 2 in. (51 mm) long and chalky white. Common in the intertidal zone from Canada to Florida, Gulf of Mexico, West Indies; also introduced in Washington and California. $2-$5

Atlantic rupellaria, *Rupellaria typica* Jonas Sometimes classified as *Petricola typica*. About 1½ in. (38 mm) long, this strong shell is grayish white, plump with coarse ribs. Common, found burrowed in coral in shallow water from North Carolina to Florida and to the West Indies. $2-$3

Surf Clams (family: *Mactridae*)

Members of this family are equivalve, usually gape slightly at the ends, and have a spoon-shaped cavity in the strong hinge. The cavity (chondrophore) holds a cartilaginous ligament (the resilium) which keeps the shells slightly separated.

smooth duck clam, *Labiosa lineata*   Say Also classified as *Anatina anatina*, Spengler. The shell is off-white, 3 in. (76 mm) long, gapes at the posterior end which has a distinct rib radiating from the beaks. The periostracum is thin, yellowish. Uncommon, found from North Carolina to Florida and Texas. $1-$2

channeled duck clam, *Labiosa plicatella* Lamarck   Also classified as *Anatina canaliculata*, Say, and in genus *Raeta*, Gray. This thin, somewhat fragile shell is white or cream, 2-3 in. (51-76 mm) long, and has concentric ribs. Common, found in sand in moderately shallow water from North Carolina to Florida, Texas, the West Indies. $1 or less

common rangia, *Rangia cuneata*   Gray Rather triangular in shape, this shell is thick, grayish white with a grayish-brown periostracum and is 1-2 in. (25-51 m) long. Common,

found in brackish water from Maryland to Florida and Texas.   under $1

Atlantic surf clam, *Spisula solidissima*, Dillwyn   Also classified as *S. raveneli*, Conrad. A large yellowish-brown shell, it reaches a length of 7 in. (178 mm), and has a thin olive-tan periostracum. Common, found in sand in moderately shallow water from Nova Scotia to Florida. This is the largest northeast coast bivalve and it is eaten. $1-$2

A smaller, southern subspecies exists, *S. s. similis*, Say. $1-$2

Pacific gaper clam, *Tresus nuttalli*,   Conrad Another large clam, it reaches 7½ in. (190 mm) in length, has a large gap through which it extends its siphons. It is yellowish white with a brown periostracum. Common, found in mud in moderately shallow water from Puget Sound to Baja California. $12-$13

Tellins (family: *Tellinidae*)

Most of the shells in this family are colorful and highly polished, and are rounded to elongate in shape. They are sand burrowers and are distinguished by a long slender siphon which is used to extract detritus from the water; another short siphon eliminates waste.

Faust tellin, *Arcopagia fausta*,   Pulteney Also listed as *Tellina fausta*. The white shell is rather heavy, has coarse growth lines and reaches a length of 4 in. (102 mm). It is a favorite food of octopuses. Common, found in moderately shallow water from North Carolina to Florida and to the West Indies. $1

Baltic macoma, *Macoma balthica* Linné A thin shell, ¾-1½ (19-38 mm) long, exterior is dull white and has a thin pale gray-brown periostracum. Common in muddy bays and coves in shallow water from the Arctic to Georgia, and the Baltic Sea to California. under $1-$3

constricted macoma, *Macoma constricta* Bruguière   This white shell has a thin, light

yellow-tan periostracum and is 2 in. (51 mm) long. Common, in shallow water from Florida to Texas and the West Indies. $1-$2

white sand macoma, *Macoma secta* Conrad A thin, glossy cream colored shell, oval shaped, it reaches a length of 4 in. (102 mm). Common, found in sand from the intertidal zone to moderately shallow water from Vancouver Island to Baja California. $1

crenulate tellin, *Phylloda squamifera* Deshayes   This white or yellowish shell has a sculpture of fine, sharp concentric ridges and thorn-like crenulations on the posterior dorsal margin. It is 1 in. (25 mm) long, fairly common in sand in moderately shallow water from North Carolina to Florida. $2-$3

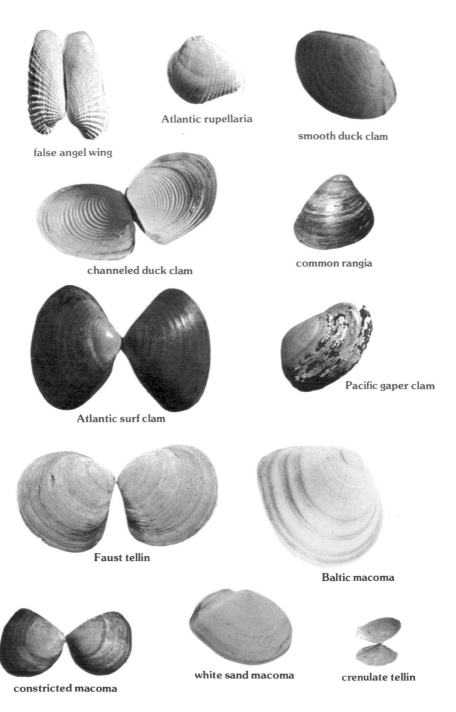

false angel wing

Atlantic rupellaria

smooth duck clam

channeled duck clam

common rangia

Atlantic surf clam

Pacific gaper clam

Faust tellin

Baltic macoma

constricted macoma

white sand macoma

crenulate tellin

Tellins (continued)

Atlantic grooved macoma, *Psammotreta intastriata* Say   Previously classified as *Apolymetis intastriata.* The shell is thin but strong, has a twisted appearance and is white, occasionally with a yellow cast. It is 3 in. (76 mm) long, moderately common, found in shallow water from Florida to the West Indies. $1-$5

rosy strigilla, *Strigilla carnaria* Linné The exterior of the shell is a pale rose, with the color deepening at the beaks; the interior is rosy pink. The shell is under 1 in. (25 mm) long, rather solid and circular in outline. This is a common species, found in shallow water from North Carolina to Florida and to the West Indies.   under $1

white-crested tellin, *Tellidora cristata* Récluz   Easily identified by the large sawteeth along the dorsal margin, this tellin is rather triangular in shape, white, and 1 in. (25 mm) long. Uncommon, found in mud or sand in shallow water from North Carolina to Florida and to Texas. $1-$2

alternate tellin, *Tellina alternata* Say An oblong shell 2-3 in. (51-76 mm) long, the surface has many parallel, fine, concentric growth lines. The color is usually white or cream, but the shell may be pink or yellow. Common, found in shallow water from North Carolina to Florida and to southern Texas. $1

crystal tellin, *Tellina cristallina* Spengler This thin, translucent white shell has concentric lines on the surface, and the posterior ends in a square-shaped upturned tip. It is 1 in. (25 mm) long, uncommon, found in moderately deep water from South Carolina to Florida and to the West Indies; Gulf of California. $2-$3

smooth tellin, *Tellina laevigata* Linné Surface of the shell is smooth, often glossy, white with pale orange rays. It is 2-3 in. (51-76 mm) long and the posterior end is bluntly pointed. Uncommon, found in shallow water from Florida to the West Indies. $7

rose petal tellin, *Tellina lineata* Turton The exterior of this shell is white, often tinged with yellow or rosy pink, with a darker shade at the beaks; interior may be pink, white, or white tinged with pink or yellow. It is ⅝-1½ in. (16-38 mm) long and the surface has fine concentric lines. Common, used in shellcraft for flower petals, it is found in shallow water from Florida to the West Indies.   under $1-$2

speckled tellin, *Tellina listeri* Röding Previously classified as *Tellina interrupta,* Wood. Exterior of this shell is white, usually with streaks of purplish brown. It is long and thin, 1-2 in. (25-51 mm) long, and has strong, regularly spaced concentric growth lines. Common, found in shallow water from North Carolina to Florida and to the West Indies; Brazil. $1-$4

great tellin, *Tellina magna* Spengler This species is our largest tellin, reaching a length of 4½ in. (102 mm). The left valve is white and not as rough as the more colorful right valve which is yellowish or orange and has fine concentric lines. Uncommon, found in shallow water from North Carolina to Florida and the West Indies. $10

sunrise tellin, *Tellina radiata* Linné This creamy white shell has rose colored bands radiating from the beaks which are also usually visible on the interior. It reaches a length of 3 in. (76 mm) and the surface is very glossy. Common, in shallow water from southern Florida to the West Indies. under $1-$5

A plain whitish or yellowish form exists, *T. r. unimaculata,* Lamarck, which lacks the colorful bands. $3-$4

salmon tellin, *Tellina salmonea* Carpenter Also classified as *T. nuculoides.* A small shell, ½ in. (13 mm) long, somewhat triangular, it has a white shiny surface with irregular purplish or reddish-brown concentric growth lines. Interior is salmon-pink. Common, in sand from shallow to moderately deep water from Alaska to California. $1 or less

candy-stick tellin, *Tellina similis* Sowerby The shell is whitish with short reddish radiating rays, fine concentric growth lines, and is thin and compressed and 1 in (25 mm) long. Common, found from the intertidal zone to moderately shallow water from southern Florida to the West Indies. $1 or less

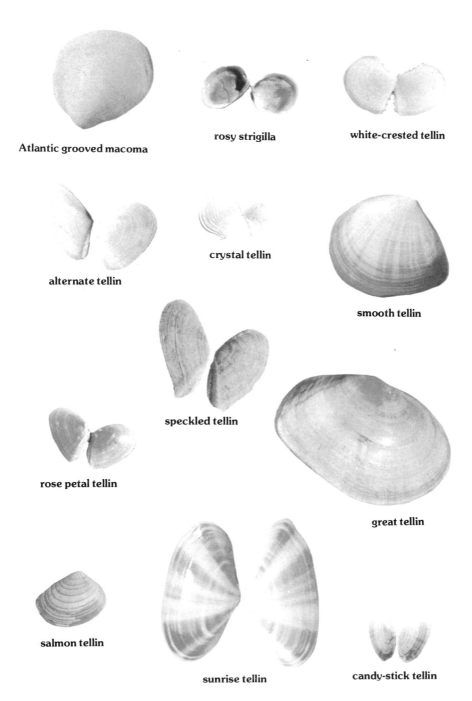

Atlantic grooved macoma

rosy strigilla

white-crested tellin

alternate tellin

crystal tellin

smooth tellin

speckled tellin

rose petal tellin

great tellin

salmon tellin

sunrise tellin

candy-stick tellin

tellins

Bean Clams and Coquinas (family: *Donacidae*)

These clams are generally wedge shaped, having an elongated and rounded posterior end and a short, sharply sloping anterior end. They live burrowed just below the surface of the sand on slopes of beaches where they move with the tide, so that they remain in the ideal wave washed area.

Caribbean coquina, *Donax denticulata* Linné   This 1 in. (25 mm) long sturdy shell varies in color from brown, violet, or yellow, may have darker rays, and has fine radiating lines on the surface. Common, found in shallow water in the West Indies.   under $1

Gould's donax or **bean clam,** *Donax gouldii* Dall   A wedge-shaped clam about 1 in. (25 mm) long, the color varies from white to purple, usually with pink or violet rays; surface has light radiating lines. Common, in intertidal area from southern California to Mexico.   under $1

Florida coquina or **common coquina,** *Donax variabilis* Say   The color of this clam is extremely variable: they may be white, yellow, pink, purple, red; they may have dark rays or concentric colored lines—or both—producing a plaid pattern. The shell is ½-¾ in. (13-19 mm) long, very common, found in the intertidal area from Virginia to Florida and Texas.   under $1

giant false coquina, *Iphigenia brasiliensis* Lamarck   This buff colored shell is purplish near the beaks, has a tan periostracum; it is heavy and reaches 3 in. (76 mm) in length. Moderately common, found in sand in shallow water from Florida to the West Indies and Brazil. $2-$3

Sanguin Clams (family: *Sanguinolariidae*)

Members of this family are shallow-water species with long separate siphons, and the shells gape at the siphonal end. Small hinge teeth are present and the large, strong ligament is external. The clams burrow and are found in mud near mangroves or in brackish water.

gaudy asaphis, *Asaphis deflorata* Linné   This is a thin, strong shell, 2 in. (51 mm) long with many radiating lines and wavy growth lines. Color is variable: most specimens are purple, but they can be white, yellow or orange. Fairly common, found from southern Florida to the West Indies.   under $1-$2

purplish tagelus, *Tagelus divisus* Spengler   The elongated, thin shell is fragile, 1-1½ in. (25-38 mm) long, and the surface is smooth and shiny. The shell is purplish gray with light purple rays; it has a thin yellowish-brown periostracum; interior purple. Common, Massachusetts to Florida, Texas, West Indies.   under $1

stout tagelus, *Tagelus plebeius* Lightfoot   This elongated shell is 3-4 in. (76-102 mm) long, gapes, and the surface has fine, concentric wrinkles. Fresh specimens are white or yellowish with a thin yellowish-brown periostracum; dead shells are white. Common, Massachusetts to Florida, Texas.   under $1

Semeles (family: *Semelidae*)

The semeles are roundish, only slightly inflated, have long separate siphons, and a large blunt foot without a byssus. They have an external ligament and a chitinous resilium. These bivalves are found in sand or mud, usually in shallow water, although some species are found in deep water. They are good eating but are not harvested commercially.

southern cumingia, *Cumingia antillarum* d'Orbigny   Also listed as *C. coarctata.* Small, white oval shell is only ⅜ in. (10 mm) long, and has irregular concentric ridges on the surface. Fairly common, found in moderately shallow water from southern Florida to the West Indies. $1-$2

cancellate semele, *Semele bellastriata* Conrad   The surface of this shell has both radiating and concentric lines; the color varies and can be yellowish tan with brownish marks or purplish gray. It is ½-1 in. (13-25 mm) long, and the shiny interior often is yellow or violet. Fairly common in moderately shallow water from North Carolina to Florida and the West Indies. $1-$2

bark semele, *Semele decisa* Conrad   A heavy large shell, it is 2-4 in. (50-102 mm) long, brownish white tinged with purple, and has coarse concentric wrinkles and a thin brownish periostracum. Dead specimens, lacking the periostracum, will be pinkish brown. Common, found on rocky bottoms in moderately shallow water from southern California to Baja California. $4

purplish semele, *Semele purpurascens* Gmelin   The shell is oval, 2 in. (51 mm) long, variable in color—pale yellow blotched with purple, brown or orange. Surface has fine concentric lines. Common, found in shallow water from North Carolina to Florida and to the West Indies. $1-$2

102

Caribbean coquina

Gould's donax

Florida coquina

giant false coquina

gaudy asaphis

purplish tagelus

stout tagelus

southern cumingia

cancellate semele

bark semele

purplish semele

bean clams / coquinas / sanguin shells / semeles

103

Jackknife Clams and Razor Clams (family: Solenidae)

The clams in this family are equivalve and generally gape at both ends. The elongated species are the jackknife clams, and the razor clams are the broader species. They are found in sandy bottoms in coastal waters. All are edible.

small jackknife clam, Ensis minor Dall This shell reaches a length of no more than 4 in. (102 mm) is quite fragile, and the whitish shell is curved and has a brown or green periostracum. Fairly common, found in the intertidal zone from Florida to Texas. $3

Many consider this shell to be a subspecies of the larger, Atlantic jackknife clam, E. directus, Conrad. $3-$5

corrugated razor clam, Solecurtus cumingianus Dunker About 1-2 in. (25-51 mm) long, this shell gapes, is rectangular, whitish with a grayish-brown periostracum. Uncommon, found in moderately deep water from North Carolina to Florida and Texas. $3-$5

green jackknife clam, Solen viridis Say This thin, elongated shell gapes at both ends, is 2-3 in. (51-76 mm) long and has a shiny greenish periostracum. Fairly common, found in intertidal zone from Rhode Island to northern Florida and northern Gulf of Mexico. under $1-$2

Geoduck Clams (family: Hiatellidae)

Valves of these clams are usually unequal and lack color; some are extremely large. These bivalves bore into sponges, coral and other limestone deposits, but some bury themselves in deep mud.

Atlantic geoduck, Panopea bitruncata Conrad The valve surfaces bear coarse, wavy growth lines and the shell is dull white. It is 4-6 in. (102-152 mm) long, has large siphons and is very similar to the larger Pacific geoduck. An uncommon species, at one time believed to be extinct; found in moderately shallow water from North Carolina to Florida. $6-$10

Pacific geoduck, Panopea generosa Gould This is the largest American clam, reaching 8 in. (203 mm) in length. The siphons are large and may stretch to 2 feet (.6 m) and cannot be completely withdrawn. The surface has concentric, wavy growth lines and has dull grayish white. Excellent food, some states have a 3-clam-daily limit. Common, in mud from Alaska to Baja California. $18

Soft-shelled Clams (family: Myacidae)

These clams usually have unequal valves that gape, with the left valve containing a spoon-like chondrophore.

soft-shell clam or **steamer clam,** Mya arenaria Linné Dull tan or grayish, this shell is 1-6 in. (25-152 mm) long, and lives buried in sand or mud with the tips of the siphons exposed. It is a popular food clam and is fished commercially. Common, found in gravel and mud in the intertidal area from Labrador to North Carolina. under $1

truncate soft-shell clam, Mya truncata Linné The posterior end of this shell is truncated and gapes prominently. The shell is 1-3 in. (25-76 mm) long, is dull white with a tough yellowish-tan periostracum. Common from the Arctic Sea to Massachusetts and to Washington on the west coast. $1

Angel Wings (family: Pholadidae)

These clams can bore into wood, coral, moderately hard rocks, as well as clay and mud. The thin, white shells are brittle, gape at both ends and have a rough abrading sculpture at the anterior end.

fallen angel wing, Barnea truncata Say The posterior end of this shell is truncated; it is white, 2-2½ (51-64 mm) long, extremely fragile and gapes widely. The surface of the valves has longitudinal and transverse wrinkles. Common, found buried in mud in the intertidal zone from Massachusetts to Florida. $1-$2

angel wing, Cyrtopleura costata Linné Previously classified as Barnea costata. This moderately fragile shell is 5-7 in. (127-178 mm) long, has widely gaping valves which touch only at the tip near the top, and has well-developed radial ribs and concentric ridges. Live specimens have a pale gray periostracum; the shell is usually pure white, but a rare pink-stained form exists. This is a fairly common species, but is subject to over-collecting. Colonies are found in mud in shallow water from Massachusetts to Florida and Texas and to the West Indies. $4-$9

campeche angel wing, Pholas campechiensis Gmelin This thin shell is greatly elongated, 4 in. (102 mm) long, white with distinct ribs. Uncommon, single valves are most often found since specimens are rarely collected alive. Found burrowed deep in mud in intertidal zone from North Carolina to Florida and the Gulf States, and to the West Indies, Brazil. $10-$30

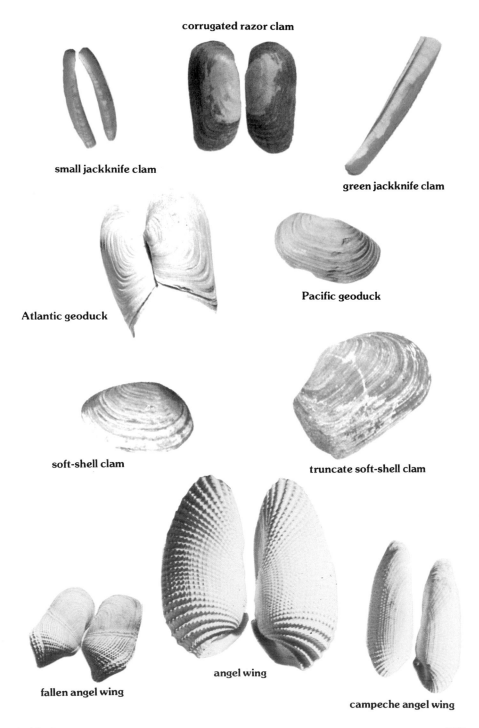

corrugated razor clam

small jackknife clam

green jackknife clam

Atlantic geoduck

Pacific geoduck

soft-shell clam

truncate soft-shell clam

angel wing

fallen angel wing

campeche angel wing

Index

* indicates photo

A

abalones 16
Acmaea limatula 18, 19*
Acmaedidae 18, 19*
Adele's nutmeg 66, 67*
Aequipecten gibbus 84, 85*
Aequipecten glyptus 84, 85*
Aequipecten irradians 84, 85*
Aequipecten irradians ampli-
  catus 84, 85*
Aequipecten irradians concen-
  tricus 84
Aequipecten irradians irradians
  84, 85*
Aequipecten lineolaris 84, 85*
Aequipecten muscosus 84, 85*
Aequipecten phrygium 84, 85*
alphabet cone 70, 71*
alternate tellin 100, 101*
American star shell 22, 23*
Americardia biangulata 94
Americardia media 94
Amphineura 5
Anadara brasiliana 78, 79*
Anadara lienosa floridana
  78, 79*
Anadara notabilis 78, 79*
Anadara ovalis 78, 79*
Anadara secticostata 78
Anodontia schrammi 90
Anatina anatina 98
Anatina canaliculata 98
Ancistrosyrinx elegans 72, 73*
angel wings 104, 105*
angular triton 42, 43*
Anodontia alba 90, 91*
Anodontia philippiana 90, 91*
Anomalocardia cuneimeris
  96, 97*
Anomia simplex 88, 89*
Anomiidae 88, 89*
Antigona rigida 96, 97*
Antigona rugatina 96, 97*
Antigona strigillina 96, 97*
Antillean scallop 86, 87*
Apolymetis intastriata 100
apple murex 48, 49*
apple seed erato 36, 37*
Arca imbricata 78, 79*
Arca umbonata 78
Arca zebra 78, 79*
Architectonica nobilis 30, 31*

Architectonica peracuta
  30, 31*
Architectonicidae 30, 31*
Arcidae 78, 79*
Arcinella arcinella 92
Arcinella cornuta 92
Arcopagia fausta 98, 99*
Arctica islandica 90, 91*
arctic clams 78, 79*
Arcticidae 90, 91*
Arene cruentata 22, 23*
Argonauta argo 76, 77*
Argonauta hians 76, 77*
ark shells 78, 79*
arrow dwarf triton 52, 53*
Asaphis deflorata 102, 103*
Astarte borealis 90, 91*
Astartidae 90, 91*
astartes 90, 91*
Astraea americana 22, 23*
Astraea caelata 24, 25*
Astraea longispina 24, 25*
Astraea longispina spinulosa
  24
Astraea phoebia 24, 25*
Astraea phoebia spinulosa
  24, 25*
Astraea tecta americana 22
Astraea tuber 24, 25*
Atlantic bay scallop 84, 85*
Atlantic carrier shell 32, 33*
Atlantic deep-sea scallop
  86, 87*
Atlantic deer cowry 36, 37*
Atlantic distorsio 44, 45*
Atlantic geoduck 104, 105*
Atlantic gray cowry 36, 37*
Atlantic grooved macoma
  100, 101*
Atlantic hairy triton 42, 43*
Atlantic jackknife clam 104
Atlantic modulus 32, 33*
Atlantic nut shell 78, 79*
Atlantic partridge tun 44, 45*
Atlantic pearl oyster 82, 83*
Atlantic rupellaria 98, 99*
Atlantic spiny oyster 88, 89*
Atlantic strawberry cockle
  94, 95*
Atlantic surf clam 98, 99*
Atlantic wing oyster 82, 83*
Atlantic wood louse 40, 41*
Atlantic yellow cowry 36, 37*
Atrina rigida 82, 83*

Atyidae 74, 75*
augers 72, 73*
Auriniopsis kieneri 64
Austin's cone 68, 69*

B

baby's ear 38, 39*
banded tulip 56, 57*
Baltic macoma 98, 99*
Barbados keyhole limpet
  18, 19*
Barbados miter 62, 63*
Barbatia cancellaria 78, 79*
Barbatia candida 78, 79*
Barbatia tenera 78, 79*
bark semele 102, 103*
Barnea costata 104
Barnea truncata 104, 105*
Beau's murex 46, 47*
beaded periwinkle 28, 29*
beaded venus 96, 97*
bean clams 102, 103*
Beau's murex 46, 47*
Benedict's scallop 84
Bequaert's murex 46, 47*
bittersweet clams 80, 81*
black clam 90, 91*
black limpet 18, 19*
black murex 48, 49*
bleeding tooth 26, 27*
blood ark 78, 79*
bonnet shells 40, 41*
boreal astarte 90, 91*
boring turret shell 30, 31*
Brachidontes exustus 80, 81*
Brachidontes recurvus 80, 81*
Branham's tulip 56, 57*
broad-ribbed cardita 90, 91*
brown crown conch 54
brown moon shell 38, 39*
brown paper nautilus 76, 77*
brown-banded wentletrap
  32, 33*
brown-lined latirus 56, 57*
brown lined paper bubble shell
  74, 75*
brown crown conch 54
brown moon shell 38, 39*
brown paper nautilus 76, 77*
bubble shell 74, 75*
Buccinum 52, 53*
Buccinum undatum 52, 53*
Bulla amygdala 74, 75*
Bulla gouldiana 74, 75*

Bullidae 74, 75*
Burry's cone 68, 69*
Bursa corrugata 44, 45*
Bursa granularis 44, 45*
Bursidae 44, 45*
Busycon carica 54
Busycon carica eliceans 54, 55*
Busycon coarctatum 54, 55*
Busycon canaliculatum 54, 55*
Busycon carica 54
Busycon carica eliceans 54, 55*
Busycon coarctatum 54, 55*
Busycon contrarium 54, 55*
Busycon pyrum 54
Busycon spiratum 54, 55*
buttercup lucine 90, 91*
buttercups 90, 91*

C

cabbage murex 46, 47*
Cabrit's murex 46, 47*
Caillet's murex 46, 47*
calico clam 96, 97*
calico scallop 84, 85*
California bubble shell 74, 75*
California cone 68, 69*
California frog shell 44, 45*
California horn shell 32, 33*
California mussel 80, 81*
Californian lucine 90, 91*
Calliostoma bonita 20, 21*
Calliostoma canaliculatum
  20, 21*
Calliostoma euglyptum 20, 21*
Calliostoma iris 20, 21*
Calliostoma javanicum 20, 21*
Calliostoma jujubinum 20, 21*
Calliostoma ligatum 20, 21*
Calliostoma supragranosum
  20, 21*
Callista eucymata 96, 97*
Calyptraeidae 32, 33*
campeche angel wing 104, 105*
Cancellaria conradiana 66, 67*
Cancellaria reticulata 66, 67*
Cancellaria reticulata adelae
  66, 67*
Cancellariidae 66, 67*
cancellate cantharus 52, 53*
cancellate semele 102, 103*
candy-stick tellin 100, 101*
Cantharus auritula 52, 53*
Cantharus cancellaria 52, 53*
Cantharus ringens 52, 53
cantharus shells 52, 53*
Cantharus tinctus 52, 53*
Cardiidae 92, 93*, 94, 95*
Cardita floridana 90, 91*
carditas 90, 91*
Carditidae 90, 91*
Caribbean carrier shell 32, 33*
Caribbean coquina 102, 103*
Caribbean olive 60, 61*
Caribbean spiny jewel box
  92, 93*
Caribbean vase shell 62, 63*
Carolina marsh clam 90, 91*

carrier shells 32, 33*
carrot cone 68, 69*
carved star shell 24, 25*
Cassidae 40, 41*
Cassis flammea 40, 41*
Cassis madagascariensis
  40, 41*
Cassis tuberosa 40, 41*
cat's paws 88, 89*
Cellana exarata 18, 19*
Cephalopoda 6
Ceratostoma nuttalli 46, 47*
Cerithidea californica 32, 33*
Cerithidea montagnei 32, 33*
chalky buttercup 90, 91*
Chama arcana 92
Chama macerophylla 92, 93*
Chama pellucida 92, 93*
Chama sinuosa 92, 93*
Chamidae 92, 93*
chank shells 62, 63*
channeled dog whelk 50, 51*
channeled dogwinkle 50, 51*
channeled duck clam 98, 99*
channeled solarielle 22, 23*
channeled top shell 20, 21*
channeled turban 24, 25*
channeled whelk 54, 55*
Charonia tritonis 42
Charonia tritonis nobilis 42
Charonia variegata 42, 43*
cherrystone clam 96
chestnut cowry 36, 37*
chestnut latirus 56, 57*
chestnut turban 24, 25*
Chione californiensis 96, 97*
Chione cancellata 96, 97*
Chione granulata 96, 97*
Chione intapurpurea 96, 97*
Chione latilirata 96, 97*
Chione mazycki 96, 97*
Chione paphia 96, 97*
Chiton tuberculatus 76, 77*
Chitonidae 76, 77*
chitons 76, 77*
Chlamys benedicti 84
Chlamys hastata 84, 85*
Chlamys imbricatus 84, 85*
Chlamys mildredae 84, 85*
Chlamys ornatus 84, 85*
Chlamys sentis 84, 85*
chocolate-lined top shell 20, 21*
Cittarium pica 20, 21*
Clark's cone 68, 69*
clear jewel box 92, 93*
cloudy periwinkle 28, 29*
Clinocardium nuttalli 92, 93*
cockles 92, 93*, 94, 95*
Codakia californica 90, 91*
Codakia orbicularis 90, 91*
coffee bean snail 74, 75*
coffee bean trivia 36, 37*
Collisella limatula 18
colorful Atlantic natica 38, 39*
Colubraria lanceolata 52, 53*
Colubraria testacea 52, 53*
Columbella mercatoria 50, 51*
Columbellidae 50, 51*

common Atlantic baby's ear
  38, 39*
common Atlantic margin shell
  66, 67*
common Atlantic slipper shell
  32, 33*
common auger 72, 73*
common blue mussel 80, 81*
common California venus
  96, 97*
common coquina 102
common dove shell 50, 51*
common European periwinkle
  28, 29*
common heart cockle 92, 93*
common northern whelk
  52, 53*
common nutmeg 66, 67*
common prickly periwinkle
  28, 29*
common purple sea snail
  32, 33*
common rangia 98, 99*
common sundial 30, 31*
common West Indian chiton
  76, 77*
common worm shell 30, 31*
conchs 34, 35*
cone shells 68, 69*, 70, 71*
Conidae 68, 69*, 70, 71*
constricted macoma 98, 99*
Conus austini 68, 69*
Conus californicus 68, 69*
Conus clarki 68, 69*
Conus daucus 68, 69*
Conus floridanus 68, 69*
Conus floridanus burryae
  68, 69*
Conus floridanus floridensis
  68, 69*
Conus granulatus 68, 69*
Conus jaspideus 68, 69*
Conus juliae 68, 69*
Conus mus 68, 69*
Conus peali 68, 69*
Conus pennaceus 68, 69*
Conus perplexus 70, 71*
Conus princeps 70, 71*
Conus pygmaeus 70, 71*
Conus ranunculus 70, 71*
Conus regius 70, 71*
Conus regularis 70, 71*
Conus sennottorum 70, 71*
Conus sozoni 70, 71*
Conus spurius atlanticus
  70, 71*
Conus spurius aureofasciatus
  70
Conus spurius spurius 70
Conus stimpsoni 70, 71*
Conus verrucosus 70, 71*
coon oyster 88, 89*
Cooper's turret shell 30, 31*
Coralliophila costata 50, 51*
Coralliophila deburghiae
  50, 51*
Coralliophilidae 50
Coralliophila abbreviata 50, 51*

Coralliophila costata 50, 51*
Coralliophila deburghiae 50, 51*
Coralliophilidae 50
Corbiculiidae 90, 91*
coral shells 50, 51*
corrugated abalone 16, 17*
corrugated razor clam 104, 105*
coquinas 102, 103*
Coue's spindle 58, 59*
cowries 36, 37*
crassatellas 90, 91*
Crassitellidae 90, 91*
Crassispira sanibelensis 72, 73*
Crassostrea gigas 88, 89*
Crassostrea virginica 88, 89*
crenulate tellin 100, 101*
crested oyster 88, 89*
Crepidula fornicata 32, 33*
cross-barred venus 96, 97*
cross-hatched lucine 90, 91*
crown conchs 54, 55*
crown cone 70, 71*
Crucibulum auricula 32, 33*
crystal tellin 100, 101*
Cumingia antillarum 102, 103*
Cumingia coarctata 102
cup-and-saucer limpets 32, 33*
cut-ribbed ark 78, 79*
Cymatiidae 42, 43*, 44, 45*
Cymatium caribbaeum 42, 43*
Cymatium chlorostomum 42
Cymatium costatum 42
Cymatium femorale 42, 43*
Cymatium krebsi 42, 43*
Cymatium martinianum 42
Cymatium muricinum 42, 43*
Cymatium nicobaricum 42, 43*
Cymatium parthenopeum 42, 43*
Cymatium pileare 42, 43*
Cymatium poulseni 42, 43*
Cymatium tigrinus 42, 43*
Cymatium vespaceum 42, 43*
Cyphoma gibbosum 36, 37*
Cyphoma mcgintyi 36, 37*
cyphoma snails 36, 37*
Cypraea cervus 36, 37
Cypraea cinerea 36, 37*
Cypraea mus 36, 37*
Cypraea spadicea 36, 37*
Cypraea spurca acicularis 36, 37*
Cypraea zebra 36, 37*
Cypraecassis testiculus 40, 41*
Cypraeidae 36, 37*
Cyrtopleura costata 104, 105*

D

dark Florida cone 68, 69*
decussate bittersweet 80, 81*
delicate file shell 88, 89*
delicate giant turret 72, 73*
deltoid rock shell 50, 51*
Diodora aspera 16, 17*
Diodora listeri 16, 17*
Dentaliidae 76, 77*

Dentalium eboreum 76, 77*
Dinocardium robustum 92, 93*
Dinocardium robustum vanhyningi 92, 93*
distorsios 42, 44, 45*
Distorsio clathrata 44, 45*
Distorsio constricta mcgintyi 44
Distorsio mcgintyi 44, 45*
Divaricella quadrisulcata 90, 91*
Doc Bale's ark 78, 79*
dog whelks 50, 51*
dog-head triton 42, 43*
dog whelks 50, 51*
dogwinkles 50, 51*
Dohrn's volute 64, 65*
Donacidae 102, 103*
Donax denticulata 102, 103*
Donax gouldii 102, 103*
Donax variabilis 102, 103*
Dosinia elegans 96, 97*
dove shells 50, 51*
drills 46, 47*, 48, 49*
dubious volute 64, 65*
dwarf hairty triton 42, 43*
dwarf tritons 52, 53*

E

eared ark 78, 79*
eastern oyster 88, 89*
eastern turret shell 30, 31*
Echininus nodulosus 26, 27*
Echinochama arcinella 92, 93*
Echinochama cornuta 92, 93*
egg cockle 94, 95*
elegant dosinia 96, 97*
elegant glassy bubble 74, 75*
elegant star turret 72, 73*
Ellobiidae 74, 75*
emperor helmet 40
empress venus 96, 97*
Ensis directus 104
Ensis minor 104, 105*
Epilucina californica 90
Epitoniidae 32, 33*
Epitonium lamellosum 32, 33*
Epitonium rupicola 32, 33*
Erato vitellina 36, 37*
Eratoidae 36, 37*
Eucrassatella speciosa 48, 49*
Eulimidae 74, 75*
Eupleura caudata 48, 49*
Eupleura muriciformis 48, 49*

F

fallen angel wing 104, 105*
false angel wing 98, 99*
false drill shell 48, 49*
false prickly-winkle 26, 27*
Fasciolaria branhamae 56, 57*
Fasciolaria hunteria 56, 57*
Fasciolaria hunteria branhamae 56
Fasciolariidae 56, 57*, 58, 59*
Faust tellin 98, 99*
file limpet 18, 19*
file shells 88, 89*

Fissurella alba 18
Fissurella barbadensis 18, 19*
Fissurella gemmata 18, 19*
Fissurella nodosa 18, 19*
Fissurellidae 16, 17*, 18, 19*
flame auger 72, 73*
flame helmet 40, 41*
flamingo tongue 36, 37*
flat oysters 82, 83*
flat tree oyster 82, 83*
Florida auger 72, 73*
Florida cone 68, 69*
Florida coquina 102, 103*
Florida crown conch 54, 55*
Florida distorsio 44, 45*
Florida fighting conch 34, 35*
Florida horse conch 58, 59*
Florida lucine 90, 91*
Florida rock shell 50, 51*
Florida spiny jewel box 92, 93*
four-spotted trivia 36, 37*
four-toothed nerite 26, 27*
frilled dogwinkle 50, 51*
frog shells 44, 45*
Fusinus couei 58, 59*
Fusinus dupetitthouarsi 58, 59*
Fusinus eucosmius 58, 59*
Fusinus halistrepus 58, 59*
Fusinus helenae 58, 59*
Fusinus timessus 58, 59*

G

Gastropoda 5
gaudy asaphis 102, 103*
gaudy cantharus 52, 53*
gaudy frog shell 44, 45*
Gaza superba 20, 21*
geoduck clams 104, 105*
giant American bittersweet 80, 81*
giant Atlantic cockle 92, 93*
giant Atlantic pyram 74, 75*
giant date mussel 80, 81*
giant eastern murex 46, 47*
giant false coquina 102, 103*
giant owl limpet 18, 19*
giant Pacific egg cockle 92, 93*
giant Pacific oyster 88, 89*
giant Pacific scallop 86, 87*
giant rock scallop 86, 87*
giant tun 44, 45*
giant white turret 72, 73*
Gibb's clam 90, 91*
glory-of-the-Atlantic cone 68, 69*
glory-of-the-sea venus 96, 97*
Glycymeridae 80, 81*
Glycymeris americana 80, 81*
Glycymeris decussata 80, 81*
Glycymeris gigantea 80, 81*
Glycymeris pectinata 80, 81*
gold-mouthed murex 46, 47*
gold-mouthed triton 42, 43*
Gould's donax 102, 103*
Gould's volute 64, 65*
granular frog shell 44, 45*
granulose top shell 20, 21*
gray Atlantic auger 72, 73*
great keyhole limpet 18, 19*

great tellin 100, 101*
green abalone 16, 17*
green jackknife clam 104, 105*
green star shell 25, 25*

H
Haliotidae 16, 17*
Haliotis corrugata 16, 17*
Haliotis fulgens 16, 17*
Haliotis rufescens 16, 17*
Haminoea elegans 74, 75*
Haminoea virescens 74, 75*
hard-shelled clams 96, 97*
harp shell 62, 63*
Harpa crenata 62, 63*
Harpidae 62, 63*
Hastula hastata 72, 73*
Haustator cooperi 30
hawk-wing conch 34, 35*
helmet shells 40, 41*
hexagonal murex 48, 49*
Hexaplex brassica 46, 47*
Hexaplex erythrostomus
  46, 47*
Hexaplex regius 46, 47*
Hiatellidae 104, 105*
Hinnites giganteus 86
Hinnites multirugosus 86, 87*
hooked mussel 80, 81*
horn shells 32, 33*
horse conchs 56, 58, 59*
Hydantina vesicaria 86, 87*
Hydantinidae 74, 75*

I
imperial venus 96, 97*
incongruous ark 78, 79*
Iphigenia brasiliensis 102, 103*
Isognomon alatus 82, 83*
Isognomon listeri 82
Isognomon radiatus 82, 83*
Isognomonidae 82, 83*
ivory tusk shell 76, 77*

J
jackknife clams 104, 105*
Janthina janthina 32, 33*
janthina snails 32, 33*
Janthinidae 32, 33*
Jasper cone 68, 69*
jewel boxes 92, 93*
jingle shells 88, 89*
jujube top shell 20, 21*
Julia's cone 68, 69*
junonia 64, 65*

K
keeled sundial 30, 31*
keyhole limpets 16, 18, 19*
Kiener's volute 64, 65*
Kiener's whelk 54, 55*
king helmet 40, 41*
king venus 96, 97*
kitten's paw 88
knobbed triton 42, 43*
knobbed whelk 54
knobby keyhole limpet 18, 19*
Knorr's worm shell 30, 31*
Kreb's triton 42, 43*

L
Labiosa lineata 98, 99*
Labiosa plicatella 98, 99*
lace murex 46, 47*
lady-in-waiting venus 96, 97*
Laevicardium elatum 92, 93*
Laevicardium laevigatum
  94, 95*
Laevicardium mortoni 94, 95*
Laevicardium substriatum
  94, 95*
lamellose wentletrap 32, 33*
lamp shell 62
Latirus brevicaudatus 56, 57*
latirus infundibulum 56, 57*
Latirus mcgintyi 56, 57*
leafy jewel box 92, 93*
lemon cockle 94
Lepidochitonidae 76, 77*
lettered olive 60, 61*
Leucozonia nassa 56, 57*
Leucozonia ocellata 56, 57*
lightning whelk 54, 55*
Lima lima 88, 89*
Lima scabra scabra 88
Lima scabra tenera 88, 89*
lined bubble shells 74, 75*
lined red chiton 76, 77*
lion's paw 86, 87*
Lister's keyhole limpet 16, 17*
Lister's tree oyster 82, 83*
Lithophaga antillarum 80, 81*
Lithophaga aristata 80, 81*
little egg cockle 94, 95*
little knobby scallop 84, 85*
Littorina angulifera 26, 27*
Littorina littorea 28, 29*
Littorina nebulosa 28, 29*
Littorina obtusata 28, 29*
Littorina saxatalis 28, 29*
Littorinidae 26, 27*, 28, 29*
livid natica 38, 29*
Livona pica 20
long-spined star shell 24, 25*
Lottia gigantea 18, 19*
Lucina filosus 90, 91*
Lucina floridana 90, 91*
Lucina pectinatus 90, 91*
Lucina pensylvanica 90, 91*
lucines 90, 91*
Lucinidae 90, 91*
Lyropecten antillarum 86, 87*
Lyropecten nodosus 48, 49*

M
Macoma balthica 98, 99*
Macoma constricta 98, 99*
Macoma secta 98, 99*
Macrocallista maculata 96, 97*
Macrocallista nimbosa 96, 97*
Mactridae 98, 99*
Magilidae 50, 51*
magnum cockle 94, 95*
Margarites vorticiferus 22, 23*
margin shells 66, 67*
marginellas 66, 67*
Marginellidae 66, 67*
marsh clams 90, 91*

marsh snails 74, 75*
McGinty's cyphoma 36, 37*
McGinty's latirus 56, 57*
McGinty's murex 48, 49*
Megathura crenulata 18, 19*
Melampus coffeus 74, 75*
Melongena corona 54, 55*
Melongena melongena 54, 55*
Melongenidae 54, 55*
Mercenaria mercenaria 96, 97*
Mercenaria mercenaria
  notata 96
Mercenaria mercenaria
  texana 96
Mildred's scallop 84, 85*
measled cowry 36, 37*
milk conch 34, 35*
milk moon shell 38, 39*
miter shells 62, 63*
Mitra barbadensis 62, 63*
Mitra florida 62, 63*
Mitridae 62, 63*
Modiolus americanus 80, 81*
Modiolus tulipa 80
Modulidae 32, 33*
modulus 32, 33*
Modulus modulus 32, 33*
Monoplacophora 5
moon shells 38, 39*
Morocco natica 38, 39*
Morton's egg cockle 94, 95*
Morum oniscus 40, 41*
mossy ark 78, 79*
mouse cone 68, 69*
mouse cowry 36, 37*
Murex beaui 46, 47*
Murex bequaerti 46, 47*
Murex bicolor 46
Murex brassica 46
Murex brevifrons 46, 47*
Murex cabriti 46, 47*
Murex cailleti 46, 47*
Murex cellulosus 46, 47*
Murex cellulosus leviculus
  46, 47*
Murex chrysostoma 46, 47*
Murex florifer 46, 47*
Murex fulvescens 46, 47*
Murex mcgintyi 48, 49*
Murex nigritus 48
Murex pomum 48, 49*
Murex recurvirostris rubidus
  48, 49*
Murex recurvirostris sallasi
  48, 49*
Murex rubidus 48
Murex sallasi 48
murex shells 46, 47*, 48, 49*
Murex tryoni 48, 49*
Murex woodringi 48, 49*
Muricanthus nigritus 48, 49*
Muricidae 46, 47*, 48, 49*,
  50, 51*
Muricopsis oxytatus 48, 49*
Muricopsis zeteki 48, 49*
music volute 64, 65*
mussels 80, 81*
Mya arenaria 104, 105*

Mya truncata 104, 105*
Myacidae 104, 105*
Mytilidae 80, 81*
Mytilus californianus 80, 81*
Mytilus edulis 80, 81*

N

Nassariidae 50, 51*
Nassarius consensus 50, 51*
Nassarius fossatus 50, 51*
Nassarius hotessieri 50, 51*
nassas 50, 51*
Natica canrena 38, 39*
Natica livida 38, 39*
Natica marochiensis 38, 39*
Naticidae 38, 39*
native Pacific oyster 88, 89*
Neopolitan triton 42, 43*
Neosimnia uniplicata 36, 37*
Neptunea decemcostata
 52, 53*
Nerita peloronta 26, 27*
Nerita tessellata 26, 27*
Nerita versicolor 26, 27*
nerites 26, 27*
Neritidae 26, 27*
Neritina piratica 26, 27*
Neritina virginea 26, 27*
netted nerite 26, 27*
netted olive 60, 61*
New England neptune 52, 53*
Niso hendersoni 74, 75*
Nodilittorina tuberculata
 28, 29*
Noetia ponderosa 78, 79*
nut shells 78, 79*
nutmegs 66, 67*
northern rough periwinkle
 28, 28*
northern yellow periwinkle
 28, 29*
northeast lucine 90, 91*
Nucella canaliculata 50, 51*
Nucella lamellosa 50, 51*
Nucula proxima 78, 79*
Nuculana acuta 78, 79*
Nuculanidae 78, 79*
Nuculiidae 78, 79*
nut shells 78, 79*
nutmegs 66, 67*
Nuttall's cockle 92, 93*
Nuttall's hornmouth 46, 47*

O

obelisk shells 74, 75*
ocean quahog 90
Oliva caribaeensis 60, 61*
Oliva incrassata 60, 61*
Oliva porphyria 60,61*
Oliva reticularis 60, 61*
Oliva reticularis bollingi
 60, 61*
Oliva reticularis greenwayi
 60, 61*
Oliva reticularis olorinella
 60, 61*
Oliva sayana 60, 61*
olive shells 60, 61*

Olivella biplicata 60, 61*
Olivella nivea 60, 61*
Olividae 60, 61*
Opeatostoma pseudodon
 56, 57*
orange marginella 66, 67*
ornamented spindle 58, 59*
ornate scallop 84, 85*
Ostrea cristata 88, 89*
Ostrea equestris 88, 89*
Ostrea frons 88, 89*
Ostrea lurida 88, 89*
Ostrea permollis 88, 89*
Ostreidae 88, 89*
Ovulidae 36, 37*
oysters 88, 89*

P

Pacific gaper clam 98, 99*
Pacific geoduck 104, 105*
Pacific littleneck 96, 97*
Pacific pink scallop 84, 85*
Panopea bitruncata 104, 105*
Panopea generosa 104, 105*
paper bubble shells 74, 75*
paper nautiluses 76, 77*
paper scallop 76, 77*
Papyridea soleniformis 94, 95*
pear whelk 54, 55*
pearl oysters 82, 83*
pearled cone 68, 69*
Pecten caurinus 86, 87*
Pecten laurenti 86, 87*
Pecten papyraceus 86, 87*
Pecten raveneli 86, 87*
Pecten tereinus 86, 87*
Pecten ziczac 86, 87*
Pectinidae 84, 85*, 86, 87*
Pelecypoda 6
pen shells 82, 83*
Pennsylvania lucine 90, 91*
Periglypta listeri 96, 97*
periwinkles 26, 27*, 28, 29*
Petricola pholadiformis 98, 99*
Petricola typica 98
Petricolidae 98, 99*
Phacoides filosus 90
Phacoides pectinatus 90
Phalium cicatricosum 40, 41*
Phalium granulatum 40, 41*
Philippi's nutmeg 66, 67*
Pholadidae 104, 105*
Pholas campechiensis
 104, 105*
Phylloda squamifera 98, 99*
Pinctada radiata 82, 83*
pink abalone 16
pink conch 34
pink-mouthed murex 46, 47*
Pinnidae 82, 83*
pisa shell 52, 53*
Pisania pusia 52, 53*
pitted murex 46, 47*
Pitar dione 96, 97*
Pitar lupanaria 96, 97*
Placopecten magellanicus
 86, 87*
Pleuroploca gigantea 58, 59*

Pleuroploca reevei 58, 59*
Plicatula gibbosa 88, 89*
Plicatulidae 88, 89*
pointed nut clam 78, 79*
pointed venus 96, 97*
Polinices brunneus 38
Polinices duplicatus 38, 39*
Polinices hepaticus 38, 39*
Polinices lacteus 38, 39*
Polymesoda caroliniana
 90, 91*
Polystira albida 72, 73*
Polystira tellea 72, 73*
ponderous ark 78, 79*
Potamididae 32, 33*
Poulsen's triton 42, 43*
prickly cockle 94, 95*
prickly winkle 28, 29*
prince cone 70, 71*
princess venus 96, 97*
Protothaca staminea 96, 97*
Prunum apicinum 66, 67*
Prunum carneum 66, 67*
Prunum guttatum 66, 67*
Psammotreta intastriata
 100, 101*
Pseudoneptunea multangula
 48, 49*
Pteria colymbus 82, 83*
Pteria sterna 82, 83*
Pteriidae 82, 83*
Puperita pupa 26, 27*
purple dwarf olive 60, 61*
purplish semele 102, 103*
purplish tagelus 102, 103*
Purpura patula 50, 51*
puzzling cone 70, 71*
pyramid shells 74, 75*
Pyramidella dolabrata 74, 75*
Pyramidellidae 74, 75*

Q

quahog 96, 97*
queen conch 34, 35*
queen helmet 40, 41*
queen venus 96, 97*

R

Raeta canaliculata 98
Rangia cuneata 98, 99*
Ravenel's egg cockle 94, 95*
Ravenel's scallop 86, 87*
razor clams 104, 105*
red abalone 16, 17*
red-brown ark 78, 79*
regular cone 70, 71*
reticulated cowry helmet
 40, 41*
rigid venus 96, 97*
rock dwellers 98, 99*
rock shells 50, 51*
rooster-tail conch 34, 35*
rose murex 48, 49*
rose petal tellin 100, 101*
rosy strigilla 100, 101*
rough lima 88
rough keyhole limpet 16, 17*
rough scallop 84, 85*

rough top shell 22, 23*
royal bonnet 40, 41*
royal comb venus 96, 97*
royal Florida miter 62, 63*
royal murex 46, 47*
Rupellaria typica 98, 99*

S
salmon tellin 100, 101*
sanguin clams 102, 103*
Sanguinolariidae 102, 103*
Sanibel turret 72, 73*
Saxidomus nuttalli 96, 97*
scallops 84, 85*, 86, 87*
Scaphella cuba 64, 65*
Scaphella dohrni 64, 65*
Scaphella dubia 64, 65*
Scaphella georgiana 64, 65*
Scaphella gouldiana 64, 65*
Scaphella junonia 64, 65*
Scaphella kieneri 64, 65*
Scaphopoda 6
scissor date mussel 80, 81*
Sconsia striata 40, 41*
scorched mussel 80, 81*
Scotch bonnet 40, 41*
sculptured top shell 20, 21*
Semele bellastriata 102, 103*
Semele decisa 102, 103*
Semele purpurascens 102, 102, 103*
semeles 102, 103*
Semelidae 102, 103*
Sennott's cone 70, 71*
sentis scallop 84, 85*
shark's eye 38, 39*
shiny Atlantic auger 72, 73*
short coral shell 50, 51*
short-frond murex 46
short-tailed latirus 56, 57*
Siliquaria squamata 32, 33*
Siliquariidae 32, 33*
simnia 36, 37*
single-toothed simnia 36, 37*
Sinum maculatum 38, 39*
Sinum perspecitivum 38, 39*
slipper shells 32, 33*
slit shells 72
slit worm shells 32, 33*
small jackknife clam 104, 105*
small whelks 52, 53*
smooth Atlantic tegula 22, 23*
smooth Scotch bonnet 40, 41*
smooth duck clam 98, 99*
smooth tellin 100, 101*
smooth-edged jewel box 92, 92, 93*
soft-shell clams 104, 105*
Solariella lacunella 22, 23*
Solencurtus cumingianus 104, 104, 105*
Solen viridis 104, 105*
Solenidae 104, 105*
southern cumingia 102, 103*
southern periwinkle 26, 27*
Sowerby's paper bubble 74, 75*
Sozon's cone 70, 71*

spathate scallop 84, 85*
speckled tellin 100, 101*
spindle shells 56
spiny file shell 88, 89*
spiny lima 88
spiny oysters 88, 89*
spiny paper cockle 94, 95*
spiny vase shell 62, 63*
spirula 76, 77*
Spirula spirula 76, 77*
Spirulidae 76, 77*
Spisula raveneli 98
Spisula solidissima 98, 99*
Spisula solidissima similis 98
Spondylidae 88, 89*
Spondylus americanus 88, 89*
Spondylus gussoni 88, 89*
sponge oyster 88, 89*
spotted baby's ear 38, 39*
star arene 22, 23*
star shells 22, 23*, 24, 25*
steamer clam 104
stiff pen shell 82, 83*
Stimpson's cone 70, 71*
stout ark 78
stout tagelus 102, 103*
Strigilla carnaria 100, 101*
Strombidae 34, 35*
Strombus alatus 34, 35*
Strombus costatus 34, 35*
Strombus gallus 34, 35*
Strombus gigas 34, 35*
Strombus pugilis 34, 35*
Strombus raninus 34, 35*
suffuse trivia 36, 37*
sundials 30, 31*
sunray venus 96, 97*
sunrise tellin 100, 101*
superb gaza 20, 21*
surf clams 98, 99*

T
Tagelus divisus 102, 103*
Tagelus plebeius 102, 103*
Tampa drill shell 48, 49*
Tectarius muricatus 28, 29*
Tegula fasciata 22, 23*
Tegula rugosa 22, 23*
Tellidora cristata 100, 101*
Tellina alternata 100, 101*
Tellina fausta 98, 99*
Tellina interrupta 100
Tellina laevigata 100, 101*
Tellina lineata 100, 101*
Tellina listeri 100, 101*
Tellina magna 100, 101*
Tellina nuculoides 100
Tellina radiata 100, 101*
Tellina radiata unimaculata 100
Tellina salmonea 100, 101*
Tellina similis 100, 101*
Tellinidae 98, 99*, 100, 101*
tellins 98, 99*, 100, 101*
Tenagodus squamatus 32
ten-ridged whelk 52
tent olive 60, 61*
Terebra cinerea 72, 73*

Terebra dislocata 72, 73*
Terebra flammaea 72, 73*
Terebra floridana 72, 72*
Terebra hastata 72, 73*
Terebra strigata 72, 73*
Terebra taurinum 72, 73*
Terebridae 72, 73*
tereinus scallop 86, 87*
tessellate nerite 26, 27*
Texas quahog 96
Thaididae 50
Thais canaliculata 50
Thais deltoidea 50, 51*
Thais haemastoma floridana 50, 51*
Thais lamellosa 50
thick-lipped drill 48, 49*
thick lucine 90, 91*
thorny oyster 88
tiger lucine 90, 91*
tiger triton 42, 43*
tinted cantharus 52, 53*
Tivela mactroides 96, 97*
Tonna galea 44, 45*
Tonna maculosa 44, 45*
Tonnidae 44, 45*
Tonicella lineata 76, 77*
top shells 20, 21*, 22, 23*
Torcula acropora 30
Trachycardium egmontianum 94, 95*
Trachycardium isocardia 94, 95*
Trachycardium magnum 94, 95*
Trachycardium muricatum 94, 95*
tree oysters 82, 83*
Tressus nuttalli 98, 99*
trigonal tivela 96, 97*
Trigonicardia biangulata 94
Trigonicardia media 94, 95*
Trigonostoma tenerum 66, 67*
Triton's trumpet 42, 43*
tritons 42, 43*, 44, 45*
tritons, dwarf 52, 53*
Trivia pediculus 36, 37*
Trivia quadripunctata 36, 37*
Trivia suffusa 36, 37*
trivias 36, 37*
Trochidae 20, 21*, 22, 23*
true bubble shells 74, 75*
true limpets 18, 19*
true tulip 56, 57*
truncate soft-shell clam 104, 105*
Tryon's murex 48, 49*
Tryon's scallop 84, 85*
tulip mussel 80, 81*
tulip shells 56, 57*
tun shells 44, 45*
turbans 22, 23*, 24, 25*
Turbinella angulata 62
Turbinella scolymus 62
Turbinellidae 62
Turbinidae 22, 23*, 24, 25*
Turbo castaneus 24, 25*
Turitella acropora 30, 31*

Turitella exoleta 30, 31*
turkey wing 78, 79*
turnip spindle 58, 59*
turnip whelk 54, 55*
turret shell 30, 31*
turrets 30, 31*, 72, 73*
Turridae 72, 73*
turrids 72⁻
Turritella cooperi 30, 31*
Turritella gonostoma 30, 31*
Turritellidae 30, 31*
tusk shells 76, 77*

U

Urosalpinx cinerea 48
Urosalpinx tampaensis 48, 49

V

variable nassa 50, 51*
vase shells 62, 63*
Vasidae 62, 63*
Vasum capitellus 62, 63*
Vasum muricatum 62, 63*
Veneridae 96, 97*
Ventricolaria rigida 96
Ventricolaria rugatina 96
Vermicularia knorri 30, 31*
Vermicularia spirata 30, 31*
virgin nerite 26, 27*
Vitularia salebrosa 48, 49*
Voluta cuba 64

Voluta dohrni 64
Voluta dubia 64
Voluta georgiana 64
Voluta gouldiana 64
Voluta kieneri 64
Voluta musica 64, 65*
volutes 64, 65*
Volutidae 64, 65*
vortex margarite 22, 23*

W

warty cone 70, 71*
Washington clam 96, 97*
wavy-lined scallop 84, 85*
weathervane scallop 86
wentletraps 32, 33*
West Indian crown conch
54, 55*
West Indian cup-and-saucer
32, 33*
West Indian dwarf olive 60, 61*
West Indian fighting conch
34, 35*
West Indian murex 46, 47*
West Indian top shell 20, 21*
West Indies prickly cockle 94,
94, 95*
western ribbed top shell
20, 21*
western strawberry cockle 94
western wing oyster 82, 83*

whelks 54, 55*
whelks, small 52, 53*
white keyhole limpet 18, 19*
white sand macoma 98, 99*
white-bearded ark 78, 79*
white-crested tellin 100, 101*
white-spotted latirus 56, 57*
white-spotted marginella
66, 67*
wide-mouthed rock shell
50, 51*
Woodring's murex 48, 49*
worm shells 30, 31*

X

Xancidae 62, 63*
Xancus angulatus 62, 63*
Xenophora caribaeum 32, 33*
Xenophora conchyliophora
32, 33*
Xenophoridae 32, 33*

Y

yellow cockle 94, 95*

Z

zebra nerite 26, 27*
zigzag periwinkle 28, 29*
zigzag scallop 86, 87*